BY ALL MEANS

Ray Comfort

BRIDGE LOGOS

Newberry, FL 32669

By All Means

Bridge-Logos, Inc.
Newberry, FL 32669, USA

Edited by Gisele Mix and Lynn Copeland

Cover by Wayne Burrow

Illustrations by Trevor Horzempa

Page design and production by Genesis Group

ISBN 978-1-61036-270-2

Library of Congress Control Number: 2021947566

All emphasis within Scripture has been added by the author.

Printed in the United States of America

CONTENTS

To Brad Snow:
a good friend, a faithful
brother in Christ, and a
wonderful graphic artist

FOREWORD

If you don't have a dog, I think you should consider
getting one. Put some sunglasses on him, as I did
with Sam, and use him to reach the lost. Nothing
gets people's attention like a cute dog wearing sunglasses—and even more so when he's on a bicycle.

> Dogs have become ubiquitous in advertising
> by businesses both large and small…. Bud
> Light began using Bull Terrier Spuds Macken-
> zie in their marketing campaign almost 30
> years ago. Beer is far from the only industry to
> call on dogs to promote their products….
>
> In recent years, dogs have appeared in
> about a third of all television commercials, and
> always figure prominently in the ones appear-
> ing during the Super Bowl.[1]

In July 2021, I received a note from a fourteen-
year-old who had given a gift of sixteen dollars to
the ministry. I decided to call and thank him.

When his mom answered the phone, she whispered, "He will be *so* excited. May I put you on
speakerphone?" I then thanked the young man for
his gift, made some small talk, and asked if he would
like to say anything before I hung up. He said that he

didn't have anything to say. It was clear that it was a little overwhelming for him. In a sense, I was a stranger, and the conversation was on speakerphone with everyone listening. But then I asked, "Do you like my dog?" Suddenly, he and his siblings blurted out that they loved Sam, that they watched our YouTube channel all the time, and that they had their own dog. The mere mention of Sam instantly made me relatable. He broke the ice.

That's what a dog can do for you when you meet strangers. But whether or not you have a dog, this book will tell you how to use what you *do* have (your undiscovered gifts, tracts, your computer, your pet elephant, etc.) to reach unbelievers.

God bless you for caring about the lost.

Ray Comfort

CHAPTER 1

EVANGELISM FROM THE CROSS

The first thing that we all have to help us reach the lost is the example of Jesus. The seven last sayings spoken by Jesus before He died on the cross should be the first words on our minds every day. They teach us that we are to love our enemies and take care of our loved ones, that God knows the future, and that He doesn't always come running to help us when we think He should. They also remind us that Jesus was a human being and experienced thirst, that He knows our everyday trials, and that He is always in perfect control—even in the face of death.

His crying, "It is finished!" (John 19:30) from the cross means that we are not. We live because of the completed work of the Savior. At any time during those six long and agonizing hours on the cross, He could have given up. But He didn't.

Something else took place during that time that is of great importance. We know that the cross was the means God used to redeem a dying humanity, but did you ever consider that those six hours were also used to reach out to the unsaved? He didn't forget them. Charles Spurgeon addresses this exact point:

> My brethren, if there had ever been a time in the life of the Son of man when he might have rigidly confined his prayer to himself, without any one cavilling thereat, surely it was when he was beginning his death throes. We could not marvel, if any man here were fastened to the stake, or fixed to a cross, if his first, and even his last and all his prayers, were for support under so arduous a trial.
>
> But see, the Lord Jesus began his prayer by pleading for others [see Luke 23:34]. See ye not what a great heart is here revealed! What a soul of compassion was in the Crucified! How Godlike, how divine! Was there ever such a one before him, who, even in the very pangs of death, offers as his first prayer an intercession for others? Let this unselfish spirit be in you also, my brethren. Look not every man upon his own things, but every man also on the things of others. Love your neighbours as yourselves, and as Christ has set before you this paragon of unselfishness, seek to follow him, treading in his steps.[2]

Jesus lived for the lost, and that passion was exemplified as He was dying for them. I say this with the utmost reverence—knowing of whom I speak. Jesus, the Creator in human form, when brought to the weakness and humiliation of the cross, used what He still had to reach the lost. He used His words, knowing how far they would reach.

Let me explain what I mean by looking at what He uttered as the Roman soldiers went about the process of His cruel murder. When He said, "Father, forgive them, for they do not know what they do" (Luke 23:34), there was no livestream. This wasn't being broadcast across the land. At best, His words were probably audible for a radius of only about fifty feet. But God knows how many people down through the ages have come to the foot of the cross after reading these words in the record of Scripture or after hearing them echoed from a pulpit. How many have been deeply affected after considering the love Jesus showed to His enemies? These words don't easily fade from memory.

I have asked many unsaved people if they know any of the last words Jesus spoke on the cross, and almost without fail, they quote verbatim this saying of His. This is because it is remarkable in the truest sense of the word.

Perhaps in these words, the Light of the world shone the brightest. He had said that Heaven and earth would pass away but that His words would never pass away (see Matthew 24:35). More than two

"Father, forgive them, for they do not know what they do." (Luke 23:34)

thousand years after these words were uttered from the cross, they have found a lodging place in the hearts of hundreds of millions. This is because they are undeniable evidence that He practiced what He preached:

> "You have heard that it was said, 'You shall love your neighbor and hate your enemy.' But I say to you, love your enemies, bless those who curse you, do good to those who hate you, and pray for those who spitefully use you and persecute you, that you may be sons of your Father in heaven; for He makes His sun rise on the evil and on the good, and sends rain on the just and on the unjust." (Matthew 5:43–45)

And that wasn't the only evangelistic light that shone from His last sayings. Think of how many have been set free from the bondage of man-made religion by understanding the implications of His saying, "It is finished!"

Let's briefly recount what led up to His seven last sayings. Then we will look at how you and I can, "by all means," as Paul said (1 Corinthians 9:22), let our own light shine as we take up our cross daily, deny ourselves, and follow Him.

The Passionate Hatred

This world revels in sin. It rolls in the prodigal son's pig slop:

They were filled (permeated, saturated) with every kind of unrighteousness, wickedness, greed, evil; full of envy, murder, strife, deceit, malice and mean-spiritedness. They are gossips [spreading rumors], slanderers, haters of God, insolent, arrogant, boastful, inventors [of new forms] of evil, disobedient and disrespectful to parents, without understanding, untrustworthy, unloving, unmerciful [without pity]. Although they know God's righteous decree and His judgment, that those who do such things deserve death, yet they not only do them, but they even [enthusiastically] approve and tolerate others who practice them. (Romans 1:29–32, AMP)

The world's love for sin and its consequential hatred for God was never more evident as when the religious leaders brought Jesus to Pilate to plead for His execution. The vultures could smell His blood and salivated at the thought of the finality of His death.

In an effort to appease the anger of the religious elite, Pilate famously suggested the release of a convicted criminal. He said to them, "Whom do you want me to release to you? Barabbas, or Jesus who is called Christ?" (Matthew 27:17). But the Scriptures tell us that the chief priests and elders persuaded the multitudes that they should ask for Barabbas "and destroy Jesus" (v. 20). They had an evil agenda they were intent on fulfilling, which was nothing less than to extinguish the Light of the world.

They so seethed with evil that they preferred to free the guilty so they could condemn the innocent. That pushed Pilate into a moral dilemma:

> Pilate said to them, "What then shall I do with Jesus who is called Christ?"
>
> They all said to him, "Let Him be crucified!"
>
> Then the governor said, "Why, what evil has He done?"
>
> But they cried out all the more, saying, "Let Him be crucified!" (Matthew 27:22,23)

When Pilate asked, "What evil has He done?" they didn't answer because they couldn't. Jesus was without sin.

Two thousand years after the fact, the wicked still try to find dirt on the spotless Lamb of God. In answer to the question, "Did Jesus sin?" one dirt-seeking skeptic said:

> If we can define some sins [that] we can all agree to be sins, then it could be possible to reach a consensus on whether Jesus sinned, if the gospel events occurred as described. I suggest one sin would be willful destruction of property:
>
> When Jesus is described as sending the demons into a herd of around 2000 pigs who

drowned in the Sea of Galilee as a result (Mark 5:13).

When Jesus is described as cursing the fig tree for not bearing fruit out of season. This also involves the sin of anger.

Jesus sinned when he attacked the money-changers who were carrying out an authorised duty in the temple, necessary so that sacrifices could be offered to God.[3]

Our skeptical friend forgot to quote a very important verse: "All things were made through Him, and without Him nothing was made that was made" (John 1:3). Jesus not only owned the pigs and the fig tree, He also created them. He could therefore do anything He wished with His own property.

And who could condemn Him for clearing hypocrites from the temple? Isn't it religious hypocrisy that offends the world? They should commend rather than condemn His taking up of the whip.

Some say that He lied when He said that not a hair on the head of His disciples would perish (see Luke 21:18). But this obviously had a deeper meaning than its face value. Death would eventually come to all of His disciples. Therefore, Jesus was clearly speaking of the resurrection of the just and the unjust. And if our faith is in Jesus, not one hair of our heads will perish either, though death may take us.

Skeptics even say He stole a donkey. Let's look at the supposed theft:

When He had said this, He went on ahead, going up to Jerusalem. And it came to pass, when He drew near to Bethphage and Bethany, at the mountain called Olivet, that He sent two of His disciples, saying, "Go into the village opposite you, where as you enter you will find a colt tied, on which no one has ever sat. Loose it and bring it here. And if anyone asks you, 'Why are you loosing it?' thus you shall say to him, 'Because the Lord has need of it.'"

So those who were sent went their way and found it just as He had said to them. But as they were loosing the colt, the owners of it said to them, "Why are you loosing the colt?"

And they said, "The Lord has need of him." (Luke 19:28–34)

The Lord had need of the donkey. Again, here is the title of ownership:

The earth is the LORD's, and all its fullness, The world and those who dwell therein. (Psalm 24:1)

The Political Puppet

The Roman governor was weak, and he caved when push came to shove:

When Pilate saw that he could not prevail at all, but rather that a tumult was rising, he took water and washed his hands before the multi-

tude, saying, "I am innocent of the blood of
this just Person. You see to it."

And all the people answered and said, "His
blood be on us and on our children." (Matthew 27:24,25)

Wicked men, bereft of the slightest mercy, put
the heel to Jesus' neck. Luke gives us a little more
detail of the cruel drama:

Pilate, therefore, wishing to release Jesus, again
called out to them. But they shouted, saying,
"Crucify Him, crucify Him!"

Then he said to them the third time,
"Why, what evil has He done? I have found no
reason for death in Him. I will therefore chas-
tise Him and let Him go."

But they were insistent, demanding with
loud voices that He be crucified. And the voices
of these men and of the chief priests prevailed.
So Pilate gave sentence that it should be as
they requested. And he released to them the
one they requested, who for rebellion and
murder had been thrown into prison; but he
delivered Jesus to their will. (Luke 23:20–25)

All this was merely a readying of the canvas. God
was about to take the brush of His goodness and
give us a vivid display of His great love.

Jesus, like a lamb to the slaughter, followed His
cross to the place of His execution: "And when they
had come to the place called Calvary, there they cru-

cified Him, and the criminals, one on the right hand and the other on the left" (Luke 23:33).

The two criminals were separated. One was placed on the right hand of Jesus, and the other was placed on His left. The Scriptures tell us that the time will come when Jesus will separate other criminals who have violated God's Law. He will set some on His right hand and some on His left:

> When the Son of Man comes in His glory, and all the holy angels with Him, then He will sit on the throne of His glory. All the nations will be gathered before Him, and He will separate them one from another, as a shepherd divides his sheep from the goats. And He will set the sheep on His right hand, but the goats on the left. (Matthew 25:31–33)

These two crucified criminals are a graphic picture of the separation of the just from the wicked—those who have turned to Jesus, repented of sin, and put their trust in Him for the salvation of their souls from those who tragically die in their sins.

The thieves were fastened to a cross. All they could do was wait for death to come. Both of these men had bigger rap sheets than just common theft:

> The men who under this name [thieves] appear in the history of the crucifixion were robbers rather than thieves belonging to the lawless bands by which Palestine was at that time and afterwards infested (Josephus, *Ant.* 17:10,

8; 20:8, 10). Against these brigands every Roman procurator had to wage continual war (Josephus, *War*, 2, 13, 2). The parable of the Good Samaritan shows how common it was for them to attack and plunder travelers even on the high-road from Jerusalem to Jericho (Lu 10:30). It was necessary to use an armed police to encounter them (Lu 22:52). Often, as in the case of Barabbas, the wild robber life was connected with a fanatic zeal for freedom which turned the marauding attack into a popular insurrection (Mr 15:7). For crimes such as these the Romans had but one sentence. Crucifixion was the penalty at once of the robber and the rebel (Josephus, *War*, 2, 13, 2).[4]

The stage is now set. The curtains are drawn. The real drama is about to begin. There are three crosses on a hill outside of the main gates of Jerusalem. The participants are three men—two guilty criminals and Jesus in their midst.

In the next chapter, we will, with fear and trembling, draw close to this terrible scene and eavesdrop on what was said by these dying men.

CHAPTER 2

JESUS IN THE MIDST

The Gospels give us four perspectives of the gruesome scene that unfolded that day:

Then two robbers were crucified with Him, one on the right and another on the left.

And those who passed by blasphemed Him, wagging their heads and saying, "You who destroy the temple and build it in three days, save Yourself! If You are the Son of God, come down from the cross."

Likewise the chief priests also, mocking with the scribes and elders, said, "He saved others; Himself He cannot save. If He is the King of Israel, let Him now come down from the cross, and we will believe Him. He trusted in God; let Him deliver Him now if He will have Him; for He said, 'I am the Son of God.'"

Even the robbers who were crucified with Him reviled Him with the same thing. (Matthew 27:38–44)

With Him they also crucified two robbers, one on His right and the other on His left. So the Scripture was fulfilled which says, "And He was numbered with the transgressors." And those who passed by blasphemed Him, wagging their heads and saying, "Aha! You who destroy the temple and build it in three days, save Yourself, and come down from the cross!"

Likewise the chief priests also, mocking among themselves with the scribes, said, "He saved others; Himself He cannot save. Let the Christ, the King of Israel, descend now from the cross, that we may see and believe."

Even those who were crucified with Him reviled Him. (Mark 15:27–31)

Then one of the criminals who were hanged blasphemed Him, saying, "If You are the Christ, save Yourself and us."

But the other, answering, rebuked him, saying, "Do you not even fear God, seeing you are under the same condemnation? And we indeed justly, for we receive the due reward of our deeds; but this Man has done nothing wrong." Then he said to Jesus, "Lord, remember me when You come into Your kingdom."

And Jesus said to him, "Assuredly, I say to you, today you will be with Me in Paradise." (Luke 23:39–43)

Then the soldiers came and broke the legs of the first and of the other who was crucified with Him. But when they came to Jesus and saw that He was already dead, they did not break His legs. But one of the soldiers pierced His side with a spear, and immediately blood and water came out. (John 19:32–34)

No doubt both thieves were familiar with Jesus. This thing wasn't done in a corner (see Acts 26:26). Jesus had been hitting the headlines for years. And yet all His fame and popularity had culminated in this horrific nightmare. The darkness had overcome the light. His enemies, like hungry lions, stood at the foot of the cross and roared out their blasphemy, wagging their heads and mocking Him. They quoted His earlier words regarding His claim that if they destroyed the temple, He would build it again in just three days:

So the Jews answered and said to Him, "What sign do You show to us, since You do these things?"

Jesus answered and said to them, "Destroy this temple, and in three days I will raise it up."

Then the Jews said, "It has taken forty-six years to build this temple, and will You raise it up in three days?"

But He was speaking of the temple of His body. Therefore, when He had risen from the dead, His disciples remembered that He had said this to them; and they believed the Scripture and the word which Jesus had said. (John 2:18–22)

"Assuredly, I say to you, today you will be with Me in Paradise." (Luke 23:40–43)

The two thieves who should have empathized with Jesus instead abused and insulted Him. What a hopeless and bitter scene.

But in the darkness, a glimmer of light began to shine. One of the thieves began to fear God (see Luke 23:40). He had a change of mind about Jesus, perhaps because He was up close and personal. It was clear that Jesus didn't react like so many before Him who had been crucified. He didn't spit out curses at those who held His arms as they nailed His hands to the cross. It was as though He laid His hands willingly against the wood. Then there were those piercing words: "Father, forgive them, for they do not know what they do" (Luke 23:34).

The thief looked across to the other thief and rebuked him, which spoke of their sin and guilt and of the innocence of the Lamb. Then he turned to Jesus and said, "Lord, remember me when You come into Your kingdom." And in doing so, he found life at the very brink of his death. Jesus said to him, "Assuredly, I say to you, today you will be with Me in Paradise" (Luke 23:40–43).

The moment this man came to faith in Jesus, another separation took place. He was taken out of darkness and brought into the light. The eyes of his understanding were enlightened. No one who has an encounter with the Savior is ever the same. Like the blind man who came to Jesus, this man suddenly saw all things clearly.

Jesus also saved us from the brink of death. Now we too can reach out to other dying sinners, pleading with them to turn to Jesus.

What You Can Do

You may not have a dog you can use to help you reach the lost, but if you can sing, dance, play an instrument, speak, teach, preach, write, or produce videos, do it with all your might. If you have any sort of talent, lay it on the altar of sacrifice. If you aren't gifted, plead with God to give you one because He is the ultimate giver of gifts: "Every good gift and every perfect gift is from above, and comes down from the Father of lights, with whom there is no variation or shadow of turning" (James 1:17).

What is your passion? What consumes you above everything else? Is it some sport? Do you want to travel and see the world? Or are you secretly seeking power, prestige, or the praise of others? Or wealth and the happiness it seems to promise you? Whatever your personal passion is, it will be the fuel that will drive you to your destination. Make sure that destination is always in the perfect will of God— because everything outside of His will is just chasing the wind. It's futile in the light of eternity. Nothing else mattered to that repentant thief as he looked death in the face. It was the knowledge of his need that caused him to turn and look to the face of Jesus.

Hopefully, you have had that same realization and have turned your face to the Savior, and now you desire above all things to reach the lost. If that's the case, you can be sure you are in the will of God, and you will find your gifting. Jesus said that everyone who asks will receive:

> So Jesus answered and said to them, "Have faith in God. For assuredly, I say to you, whoever says to this mountain, 'Be removed and be cast into the sea,' and does not doubt in his heart, but believes that those things he says will be done, he will have whatever he says. Therefore I say to you, whatever things you ask when you pray, believe that you receive them, and you will have them." (Mark 11:22–24)

Now add to that the knowledge that the cross is evidence that God is the lover of your soul. You were the object of His passion on that day. Make Him the object of yours. Run to do His will. Be like the excited woman at the well. She didn't sit there and do a six-week training course on presuppositional apologetics. After she met Jesus, she *immediately* told others about Him—and look what happened:

> And many of the Samaritans of that city believed in Him because of the word of the woman who testified, "He told me all that I ever did." So when the Samaritans had come to Him, they urged Him to stay with them; and

He stayed there two days. And many more believed because of His own word.

Then they said to the woman, "Now we believe, not because of what you said, for we ourselves have heard Him and we know that this is indeed the Christ, the Savior of the world." (John 4:39–42)

Look also at a man we know only as "Legion":

When [Jesus] stepped out on the land, there met Him a certain man from the city who had demons for a long time. And he wore no clothes, nor did he live in a house but in the tombs. When he saw Jesus, he cried out, fell down before Him, and with a loud voice said, "What have I to do with You, Jesus, Son of the Most High God? I beg You, do not torment me!" For He had commanded the unclean spirit to come out of the man. For it had often seized him, and he was kept under guard, bound with chains and shackles; and he broke the bonds and was driven by the demon into the wilderness.

Jesus asked him, saying, "What is your name?"

And he said, "Legion," because many demons had entered him. And they begged Him that He would not command them to go out into the abyss. (Luke 8:27–31)

Demons had made this poor man's life a living nightmare. But Jesus cast them into pigs, who then plunged down the steep hillside and drowned in the sea. Look at what happened next:

> When those who fed them saw what had happened, they fled and told it in the city and in the country. Then they went out to see what had happened, and came to Jesus, and found the man from whom the demons had departed, sitting at the feet of Jesus, clothed and in his right mind....
>
> Now the man from whom the demons had departed begged Him that he might be with Him. But Jesus sent him away, saying, "Return to your own house, and tell what great things God has done for you." And he went his way and proclaimed throughout the whole city what great things Jesus had done for him. (vv. 34–39)

After the man met Jesus, he sat at His feet, clothed and in his right mind. He then wanted to go with Jesus, but Jesus' concern was for the salvation of the man's family. He told him, "Return to your own house, and tell what great things God has done for you."

Can you imagine what a powerful and God-glorifying testimony that would have been to this man's entire neighborhood? His had been a hopeless case of insanity and self-destruction. But he suddenly returned clothed, in his right mind, and pointing people to Jesus. He hadn't been trained in the nuances of human interaction. But like the woman at the well, he immediately began to evangelize.

We also were once out of our minds because of sin. We were self-destructive, hopeless, helpless, demon-directed, and naked before a holy God, but

> you He made alive, who were dead in trespasses and sins, in which you once walked according to the course of this world, according to the prince of the power of the air, the spirit who now works in the sons of disobedience, among whom also we all once conducted ourselves in the lusts of our flesh, fulfilling the desires of the flesh and of the mind, and were by nature children of wrath, just as the others. (Ephesians 2:1–3)

Both the woman at the well and the man known as Legion were motivated by a sense of excitement. If we understand who Jesus is and what He did for us on the cross, we too will be bursting with excitement to tell this dying world about the Savior.

In the next chapter, we will look at how we can overcome our fears, and what we can do practically to help us share the good news.

CHAPTER 3

GETTING RID OF AWKWARDNESS

The third statement Jesus made from the cross was directed toward His mother and one of His disciples:

> When Jesus therefore saw His mother, and the disciple whom He loved standing by, He said to His mother, "Woman, behold your son!" Then He said to the disciple, "Behold your mother!" And from that hour that disciple took her to his own home. (John 19:26,27)

Once again, even in the agony of the cross, Jesus is concerned for His precious mother's well-being. But He didn't commit her to His half brothers, who were not believers (see John 7:5). He committed her into the hands of John, who would love His mother with the godly love that was shed abroad in his heart.

As Christians, each of us have many brothers and sisters and mothers and fathers in the family of

"Woman, behold your son!" (John 19:26)

God. Often these spiritual relationships are deeper than the relationships we have with our own flesh-and-blood earthly family. This is why it's heartbreaking when professing Christians argue over some non-essential doctrine, or over some personal prophetic interpretation, and cause splits within the family of God. We are called to be "good" soldiers (2 Timothy 2:3), and our battle is with the world, the flesh, and the devil—not with other Christians. We exist to, with God's help, seek and save dying sinners from the terrors of a very real Hell. This is why "friendly fire" is such a tragedy. We must uphold one another's arms, as Aaron and Hur did for Moses, so that the battle can be won—not shoot each other in the back.

So if you find someone who professes faith in Jesus, but causes division, mark them and avoid them:

> Now I urge you, brethren, note those who cause divisions and offenses, contrary to the doctrine which you learned, and avoid them. For those who are such do not serve our Lord Jesus Christ, but their own belly, and by smooth words and flattering speech deceive the hearts of the simple. (Romans 16:17,18)

We have better things to do with our time, and our number one priority is to fight the good fight of faith. And that means going into the world and taking the gospel to friends, relatives, neighbors, and even strangers, so that they too can become part of the family of God. That's not an easy task, but it is a task that can be made easier.

Going Fishing

Let's say you want to deepen the fellowship of the men at your church. They hardly know each other aside from a superficial Sunday morning courtesy greeting. You could put them in one room at your church and see what happens. But if they're normal, it will be a little awkward as they introduce themselves to each other and make small talk.

The world fixes this awkwardness with alcohol. Liquor loosens the areas of the mind that are normally inhibited. However, there's a safer and easier way to get men to mingle. Simply divide them into two teams, toss a football into the middle, and watch what happens. Before you know it, they will all be buddies. This is because the ball takes the focus off each individual. It becomes the center of attention, and that gets rid of the awkwardness.

The same awkwardness often occurs when we meet a stranger. But put a dog into the mix, and the pooch takes the focus off us. He becomes the center of attention. That makes meeting strangers so much easier. That's what Sam does for me almost every day.

If you have a dog, do what I did. Drill four small holes into some sunglasses—one on each side of the glasses area, and two more holes in the arms where the glasses go over the ears. Thread two pieces of thin elastic through the holes—one through the front holes (for under the chin) and the other through the arms (for behind the head). Then put them on your dog and go for a walk, and take some gospel tracts with you (see some great tracts at LivingWaters.com[5]). Be ready to warmly greet strangers. If you do that regularly, with a little love and boldness, your life will become an adventure because you will be doing the greatest thing any human being can do. You will be collaborating with God by fishing for men and women.

Keep in mind that every now and then a fish may jump into your boat, but ordinarily you will have to drop a line or cast a net. You will have to *go* into the world to share the gospel (see Mark 16:15). I normally go out on my bike once a day. When Sam gets up on the platform and slips his head through his seatbelt, I talk to him. If you're a dog lover, you'll know that I'm not completely crazy. I look into his eyes as he looks intently into mine, and I say, "We're going out on the bike. You're going to look for cats, and I'm going to look for people with whom I can speak. Here are my sunglasses, and here are yours." And as I slip his on him, I say, "May God lead me today to someone He's prepared." This is my silly routine, but I love doing it. For some reason, talking to my dog generates a sense of adventure and focuses my intention on what we're doing.

Going out each day is a discipline that has nothing to do with my feelings. I go out if I feel full of energy, and I go out if I'm tired. I go if I want to, and I go if I don't. I have this mindset because I know I have a responsibility that is even greater than the responsibility of a firefighter. He doesn't respond to calls according to his feelings. Feelings are irrelevant. He responds because it's his duty to do so. To not respond to an emergency is abhorrent. If he isn't 100 percent committed to his duty, he has no right to call himself a firefighter. That's my daily mindset as well.

If you've got kids, take them with you when you go to give out gospel tracts and share your faith. That will make your evangelism even more meaningful because you're setting an example of where your life's priorities are. It won't be long before your kids will want to join you. We often get emails similar to the following:

> After five days of watching the grown-ups do evangelism at our county fair, my youngest son, Benny (age four), decided he wanted to give it a try. People loved it! Thank you for equipping me so that I could equip my children. —Kathryn S.

David Grantham, a pilot with US Customs and Border Protection, regularly sends me photos of people joyfully holding our tracts, along with texts such as this one:

It never ever fails. When you hand out Million Dollar Bill tracts in line at a store, every person smiles and thanks you for them. People are so grim now, and it completely lightens the mood among a group of complete strangers.

Consider these encouraging testimonies:

I'd like to thank you for producing the million-dollar tracts. Because of it, I got saved and gave my life to Jesus Christ eight years ago. I used to be an atheist and God brought me to my knees through your million-dollar tract. I went from being an atheist to being on staff at a church, and now I evangelize regularly. —Peter G.

I received a million-dollar bill at my job a month ago, and I thought it was a tip at first as it was left with the tip the customer gave me. I took it home and read it. I lost someone precious to me over two years ago. No one has ever talked to me about the afterlife or taken the time to care about me like that. We all think about death. I have never in my life understood so clearly what the "big deal" with Christianity was as after having read the bill. That's a huge deal concerning my life after death. It breaks my heart Jesus died. —Lindsey A.

Perhaps for some reason you can't get out regularly to give out tracts, but you do care for the lost. There is an effective way to fulfill that passion, and you don't even have to confront strangers. All you

need is a caring heart, a little time, and access to the
Internet. Here's what you can do. Copy the following
wording and paste it online:

> Sometimes we joke about death. But it's really
> not funny. Life is frightening enough, but
> death makes it worse. If you've ever wondered
> if there's something you can do about what the
> Bible calls "the king of terrors," there certainly
> is. And it has nothing to do with becoming
> "religious" or being a good person. If you're
> interested, simply go to NeedGod.com and see
> what you think. You'll be forever glad you did.
> Thank you for reading this.

Find a YouTube channel or anywhere on the
Internet that allows comments and drop it in. Who
knows—because you make a disciplined habit of
doing this each day, someone might find everlasting
life! Think about that for a moment, and then read
and memorize this verse: "Let him know that he who
turns a sinner from the error of his way will save a
soul from death and cover a multitude of sins"
(James 5:20).

If you prefer to give the entire gospel instead of
simply directing them to NeedGod.com, use the following text:

> THE MILLION-DOLLAR QUESTION: Will
> you go to Heaven when you die? Have you
> lied, stolen, used God's name in vain, or lusted

(which Jesus said was adultery, Mt. 5:28)? If so, God sees you as a liar, thief, blasphemer, and adulterer at heart. If you die in your sins, you will end up in a terrible place called Hell. But there's good news. Though we broke God's Law, Jesus paid the fine by dying on the cross: "God so loved the world that He gave His only begotten Son, that whoever believes in Him should not perish but have everlasting life" (Jn. 3:16). Then Jesus rose from the dead and was seen by hundreds of eyewitnesses. He fulfilled all the prophecies of the promised Savior. Please, today, repent and trust Jesus, and God will forgive you and grant you the gift of eternal life (Eph. 2:8,9). Then, to show your gratitude, read the Bible daily and obey it, join a Christian church, and be baptized. Visit NeedGod.com and LivingWaters.com.

You don't even need to type it out. Just go to LivingWaters.com and click on Store, then Tracts and Money. This is the text for our wildly popular Million Dollar Bill tract. (You have our joyful permission to use it. You are not violating any copyright laws.)

Again, keep in mind that you are fishing for men and women. Sometimes fish nibble; sometimes they take your hook, line, and sinker. Don't be discouraged when someone responds to you with a biting comment. Make sure you pray for any who respond in a negative way. You're like a dentist, probing teeth for decay, and when there is a painful reaction, you know that you're in business.

Then again, you might get positive reactions. You might find yourself talking to a penitent thief who wants to turn to Jesus—and to that person you're a godsend. Whatever the case, always keep these words in mind: "Therefore, my beloved brethren, be steadfast, immovable, always abounding in the work of the Lord, knowing that your labor is not in vain in the Lord" (1 Corinthians 15:58).

In the next chapter, we will look at the key difference between the two crucified thieves and how knowing that difference can help us to reach the lost.

CHAPTER 4

DO THEY REALLY KNOW?

The first statement Jesus made on the cross bears a closer look. When He said, "Father, forgive them, for they do not know what they do" (Luke 23:34), we see why He prayed that they receive mercy. The apostle Paul specifically addresses this:

> And I thank Christ Jesus our Lord who has enabled me, because He counted me faithful, putting me into the ministry, although I was formerly a blasphemer, a persecutor, and an insolent man; but I obtained mercy because I did it ignorantly in unbelief. And the grace of our Lord was exceedingly abundant, with faith and love which are in Christ Jesus. This is a faithful saying and worthy of all acceptance, that Christ Jesus came into the world to save sinners, of whom I am chief. However, for this reason I obtained mercy, that in me first Jesus Christ might show all longsuffering, as a pat-

tern to those who are going to believe on Him for everlasting life. (1 Timothy 1:12–16)

Jesus said that those who crucified Him didn't know what they were doing. The apostle Paul said a similar thing—what he did was done in ignorance. This is the universal state of all mankind:

This I say, therefore, and testify in the Lord, that you should no longer walk as the rest of the Gentiles walk, in the futility of their mind, having their understanding darkened, being alienated from the life of God, *because of the ignorance that is in them*, because of the blindness of their heart; who, being past feeling, have given themselves over to lewdness, to work all uncleanness with greediness. (Ephesians 4:17–19)

In a sense, the world *does* know what they are doing. They are in a love affair with sin. Saul of Tarsus, those who stoned Stephen, and those who crucified Jesus knew what they were doing. Paul hated the name of Jesus. The Pharisees hated what Stephen preached, and they were furious when Jesus cleared the temple. Jesus called them hypocrites, publicly denounced them, and highlighted their sins. They wanted Him dead. But they didn't know that He was the very Lord of glory they professed to worship (see James 2:1)—and therefore their only hope of salvation from the horror of death. If they had known that, they wouldn't have crucified Him: "But we speak the wisdom of God in a mystery, the hidden wisdom which God ordained before the ages for our glory, which none of the rulers of this age knew; *for had they known, they would not have crucified the Lord of glory*" (1 Corinthians 2:7,8).

Jesus alluded to this ignorance with the woman at the well when He said, "If you knew the gift of God, and who it is who says to you, 'Give Me a drink,' you would have asked Him, and He would have given you living water" (John 4:10).

If the world knew who Jesus is—the source of life, the only hope of immortality—they would seek after Him as desperate and dying people. But they are sorely ignorant. This is what we must always keep in mind when seeking the lost. Without empathy, we will lack a merciful attitude. And that means we will become discouraged at the first sign of the aggression that is born out of this ignorance.

Think again of the penitent thief *before* he began to fear God. If we had been privy to the conversation, it would be easy to discount him as a candidate for salvation when he was reviling and blaspheming Jesus. He was unconcerned about his salvation as well as blasphemous and anti-Christ in attitude. But something caused the fear of God to open his eyes, and unlike the other thief, he humbled himself and turned to the Savior. Look at this change. He went from blaspheming Jesus to saying to the other thief, "Do you not even fear God, seeing you are under the same condemnation?" (Luke 23:40).

There are only two real divisions among humanity—the humble and the proud. The contrast of these two categories was evident in the thieves on each side of Jesus: one was interested in this life; the other suddenly set his eyes on eternity. That's why he said, "Lord, remember me when You come into Your kingdom" (v. 42). What was the difference between the two? Why did one suddenly change, fear God, and turn to Jesus, calling Him "Lord," and the other revile Him? I believe it came about because of the differing results of pride and humility.

God has given us His blueprint for salvation. He "resists the proud, but gives grace to the humble" (1 Peter 5:5). No proud person has even gotten through the door of salvation—because it is a very low means of entry. I see this principle almost daily as I go through the Ten Commandments with people and listen to proud hearts trivialize sin. They try to justify every evil thing they do and remain blind to the gospel. Those who are humble admit their sins and don't justify themselves. They are able to see the mercy of God in Christ:

> He who covers his sins will not prosper,
> But whoever confesses and forsakes them will
> have mercy. (Proverbs 28:13)

Pride turns off the light of the gospel; it keeps sinners in darkness. Humility turns it on. The moment I detect a proud heart, I know that the good news of the gospel won't be seen or understood by that individual, and there's a commonsense reason why this so often happens.

If a proud man sits in a doctor's office and refuses to acknowledge symptoms of a terminal disease, he will be deceived into thinking he is healthy and will quickly discard a cure. Likewise, when the proud refuse to acknowledge their sins, they quickly discard the cure of the gospel. Why, then, was one thief proud and the other thief humble?

For many years I poached an egg for breakfast and ended up with an inedible white "fluff" that forms on top of the egg as it cooks. One day, for some reason, I put a lid on the pot of boiling water, and to my delight not only was the egg cooked much quicker but there was no fluff.

That's what happened to the penitent thief. The pressure of his terrifying predicament cleared his mind of fluff—the things in life that don't matter. At any moment, Roman soldiers would come, break his legs, and usher him into eternity. As he saw death approaching, nothing else was of concern but his salvation.

We long for this world to come to the Savior, but that won't happen while pride stands in the way. Pride will leave sinners like the unrepentant thief—helpless and hopeless in the face of the horror of death. Therefore, if we care, we must take courage and apply pressure. We must speak of their impending death and plague them with the moral Law, the Ten Commandments, and pray that they see what matters in life, humble themselves, and let go of their beloved sins.

It's Not Rocket Science

Following is a word-for-word witnessing encounter from our TV show, *Way of the Master*, as an example of how to lovingly apply pressure. It's a conversation with a genuine rocket scientist (who was an atheist) and three other people.

RAY: What do you do for a living?

ERIC: I am a coordinate metrology system specialist quality engineer. I contract to companies like NASA and SpaceX and build rockets and rocket engines.

RAY: Are you an atheist?

ERIC: I am.

RAY: If I could prove God scientifically to you, would you change your mind?

ERIC: You *can't* prove it scientifically.

RAY: How do you think we got here?

ERIC: We evolved from ocean creatures.

RAY: So how did the ocean creatures get here?

ERIC: They evolved from bacteria and other organisms.

RAY: How did the bacteria get here?

ERIC: Uh, two atoms collided in space.

RAY: Where did the atoms come from? They're very complex, atoms.

ERIC: Yes…everything's just always existed. I don't know where it came from.

RAY: That's scientifically impossible. The second law of thermodynamics: everything runs down. So the universe can't be eternal. It *must* have had a beginning. You're an atheist; do you believe the scientific impossibility that nothing created everything? Because that's what an atheist believes.

ERIC: Yes, but, that's what I'm saying is, where it started, you know, we consider it "nothing" because no one was there—there's no way to know what happened. We know it's constantly expanding, and that it started somewhere.

RAY: Let me ask you again. Do you believe the scientific impossibility that nothing created everything? Because that's the only alternative to God creating everything.

ERIC: No. Not "nothing created everything"; something was there.

RAY: In the beginning?

ERIC: In the beginning, yes.

VINCENT: Well, I'm reading this book right now [and] you're talking about the afterlife—*The Inferno of Dante*.

RAY: Wow! What's that about?

VINCENT: It's Hell, and it's, like, levels of Hell.

RAY (to ANNIE and MELISSA): Do you ladies think there's an afterlife?

MELISSA: Um, yes.

RAY: Where do you get your information from?

MELISSA: The Bible.

RAY: Do you think Adam and Eve were primates?

MELISSA: (chuckles) They were playmates.

RAY: Playmates? (all laugh) Are you a good person?

MELISSA: Yes.

RAY: And what about you?

ANNIE: Yes, I believe so.

RAY (to VINCENT): Where are you going when you die? Are you going to Heaven, or are you going to Dante's inferno? There's a statue called *The Thinker*. Have you ever seen it? It's a guy just leaning on his elbow, and his hand is on his chin, and he's thinking. It's very famous. It's actually taken from Dante's *Inferno*, and it's Adam looking at people going to Hell because of the original sin that he passed on to them, and that's what he's thinking about.

RAY (to ERIC): So, you're stuck with a huge dilemma. There must have been an initial cause, and you don't want to call it "God," and I think I know why. Because when we mention God, it means moral responsibility. It means pornography's wrong, adultery's wrong, sex before marriage is wrong. All the things we love are wrong, and we don't want God interfering in our lives. Am I getting close to the truth?

ERIC: I mean, I can see how you would see that's the truth, but I'm not very shy. I don't need—I mean, I know my morals are good.

RAY: How many lies have you told in your life?

VINCENT: I have told so many lies.

RAY: Ever stolen something?

ERIC: Yes.

RAY: Have you ever used God's name in vain?

VINCENT: Always.

ANNIE: Yes.

MELISSA: Yes.

ERIC: Yes.

RAY: Jesus said if you look at a woman with lust, you commit adultery with her in your heart. Have you ever looked at a woman with lust?

ERIC: Of course.

RAY: Have you had sex out of marriage?

ERIC: Yes.

RAY: Eric, I'm not judging you, but you've just told me you're a liar, a thief, a blasphemer, a fornicator, and an adulterer at heart. You have to face God on Judgment Day, whether you believe in Him or not. If He judged you by the Ten Commandments on Judgment Day, would you be innocent or guilty?

ANNIE: Guilty.

MELISSA: Guilty.

RAY (to VINCENT): So if you're guilty on Judgment Day, will you go to Heaven or Dante's inferno?

RAY (to ERIC): You'd end up in Hell, according to the Bible, and that grieves my heart. That horrifies me. I like you, and the thought of you ending up in Hell greatly disturbs me. Two thousand years ago, God became a human being, Jesus of Nazareth, a perfect sinless Man who gave His life on the cross to take the punishment for the sin of the world. You and I broke God's Law, the Ten Commandments; Jesus came and paid our fine. If you're in court and someone pays your fine, the judge can let you go. He can be just and yet show you mercy. He can say, "Look, Eric's guilty, but someone's paid his fine—he's out of here." Just before Jesus died, He called out, "It is finished!" In other words, the debt has been paid. That means God can legally dismiss your case, forgive your sins, let you walk out of the courtroom, commute your death sentence, and let you live forever—because of the death and resurrection of the Savior. What you have to do is repent and trust in Jesus, like you'd trust a parachute. You don't just believe in a parachute, you put your faith in it. Eric, the minute you do that, God will forgive every sin you've ever committed and grant you everlasting life as a free gift because He's rich in mercy.

That's the gospel. You're a space engineer, a rocket scientist. I'm not asking you to swallow those Bible stories; I'm asking you to swallow your pride and believe the gospel—simply that you're a sinner and Christ died for your sins as your substitute. If you'll repent and trust in Him, God will reveal Himself to you; you've got His promise on that. Does that make sense?

ERIC: Yes. I mean, I'm going to take the time to reread it.

RAY: Read the Gospel of John; just stay with that. The Gospel of John describes Jesus, and there's no one like Him. I mean, He said things that were just crazy, or He was God in the flesh. He said that the hour is coming when all who are in their graves will hear His voice. They're either the words of a madman, or they're the words of God.

ERIC: So you're just saying, like, there's someone following Him, writing this stuff down?

RAY: Yes, the Holy Spirit inspired men to write down what He said. So at the moment, you're up the river Niagara without a paddle. You're going to die. You're going to go over the falls one day, and you don't know when. There's only one rope being thrown to you, and that's the gospel of Jesus Christ. So please consider it, because there's nothing more important than where you'll spend eternity.

RAY (to ANNIE and MELISSA): At the moment, you ladies are trusting in your goodness to save you on Judgment Day. Well, transfer your trust from yourself to the Savior. It's like if you jump out of a plane at ten thousand feet—you don't try to save yourself by flapping your arms; it's not going to work. Trust the parachute. Has it made sense, what I've been saying to you today?

MELISSA: Yes.

RAY: You going to think about this?

ANNIE: Yes.

RAY: What about you?

MELISSA: Oh, yes, I will.

VINCENT: Yes, I'm going to think about it, and probably go to church this Sunday.

RAY (to ERIC): Well, I'm saying, if you put your faith in God, He'll never let you down. He's the Creator of the universe. No rocket you've ever made has made itself; that's ludicrous. The rocket is proof of a manufacturer, and creation is proof of a Creator. It's just common sense; a child can understand it. So will you at least think about what we talked about?

ERIC: Yes, for sure.

In the next chapter, we'll discuss seven mistakes you should avoid when witnessing to others.

CHAPTER 5

SEVEN MISTAKES YOU SHOULD AVOID WHEN WITNESSING

By far the most common question I'm asked about witnessing is how to approach a stranger with the gospel. It's all very well to speak of applying pressure to sinners, but how do we do that without being offensive? The answer is simple: ask questions. Most conversations are started with general questions—for example, "How are you?" "What's your name?" "How's your day going?" "What kind of work do you do?" "Do you live in this area?" Politely asked questions show that we care. I use them every time I share my faith. They help strangers to relax because the questions are easy for them to answer and people are usually happy to talk about themselves.

The questions are simply a means to an end. They begin in the natural realm, but our agenda is to move into the spiritual realm. I make that transition by asking, "Do you think there's an afterlife?" No matter how they respond, I follow that with, "Do you think about it much?" Each of their answers will naturally lead into more questions. One interesting question to ask is, "Do you have a bucket list?" Do they have things they plan to do before they die?

Another reason I ask questions is because this is what Jesus did. The four Gospels tell us He asked over a hundred questions. Here are some questions I have collated over the years that you may like to ask to stir conversation:

- If you could ask God for one thing, what would it be?

- Have you ever won something?

- Does money make you happy?

- How well do you sing—one to ten?

- What's the worst thing you've ever tasted?

- Do you dominate the use of the remote control?

- How many times do you look in the mirror each day?

- What's the strangest belief you held as a child?

- What are the best steps we can take to improve our health?

- Is it important to you that people remember your name?

- Are you a rule breaker or a rule keeper?

- Are you superstitious?

- What do you take for granted the most?

- Are you a risk taker?
- What fear would you like to overcome?
- What's something that amazes you?
- Do you ever have trouble sleeping?
- What person (dead or alive) would you want to be like?
- What's your favorite season of the year?
- What's your favorite holiday tradition?
- What social issues fire you up?
- What's the most dangerous situation you've encountered?
- Have you ever helped a total stranger?
- What's one of your most frightening moments?
- Do you ever have nightmares?
- If you could give one gift to your children, what would it be?
- If you could rid the world of one evil, what would it be?
- What do you fear most?
- Why do you think it's hard for people to say, "I'm sorry"?
- Do you receive criticism easily?
- What do you think was the most significant event in history?
- Do you believe in capital punishment?
- Is abortion wrong?

- What is one thing in life you know for sure?
- Have you ever been caught doing something wrong?
- Would you like to know the date and cause of your death?
- What was the hardest thing you've ever done?
- What was the most significant loss you have experienced?

When sharing the gospel, it's helpful to begin with some common questions, but there are also some common mistakes to avoid. The goal of most parents is to save their children some pain. They don't want their kids to fall into the same pitfalls they did. That's why they teach them that the toaster is hot, to avoid petting strange dogs, and to look both ways when crossing the road. Having been burned, bitten by a strange dog, or nearly hit by a car can add conviction to the parents' words.

We are going to look at seven mistakes we should avoid when witnessing to others. I share them with conviction because they are mistakes I have made in the past. They are important to know —not just for your sake but for the sake of those with whom you'll be speaking.

Don't Be Aimless

If you share your faith without knowing what you want to achieve, you are driving a car without a destination and you're going to end up lost. Your destination is that sinners understand the gospel and why they desperately need God's mercy. In the parable of the sower (Matthew 13), the good soil represents the one who hears the message and *understands* it. Without that understanding, the lost will go on in their sins. You are a firefighter who is trying to save people from a burning building. You're not there to paint their house, work in the garden, or take them a free meal. The unsaved are in great danger of going to Hell if they die in their sins. Your job isn't to say they can have an improved lifestyle if they give their heart to Jesus. When the thief on the cross turned to Jesus and put his trust in Him, he began his new life in Christ. But the first thing that happened to him after doing so was that Roman guards broke both of his legs. His life did not improve when he put his faith in Jesus. We need a Savior not for this life but for the next.

Here is our agenda when sharing with others: "On some have compassion, making a distinction; but others save with fear, pulling them out of the fire, hating even the garment defiled by the flesh" (Jude 22,23).

Avoid Rabbit Trails

While it's important to deal with subjects such as evolution, atheism, and supposed mistakes in the Bible, they should be dealt with very briefly. If you become distracted by them, you will not meet your agenda. If you see someone in a house that's on fire and they refuse to listen to you because they want to talk about the political climate or their annoying neighbors, you could perhaps give them a brief answer. But your job is to tell them their house is on fire and they must get out as soon as possible. If you go down the rabbit trail of Darwinian evolution, you will find that it is never ending. This theory is unproven, unprovable, and has nothing to do with true science. It is a fairy tale for grownups, but you won't convince a staunch believer of that fact. So avoid it. You don't need to go down that rabbit trail. It's only an issue if you make it an issue.

If you watch our videos, you will see that people who believe in evolution don't get upset when I change the subject to the gospel. That's what they need to hear. Always remember that it's the gospel that is the power of God to salvation (Romans 1:16). Don't get distracted from your agenda to fulfill the Great Commission. Neither do you need to argue about the existence of God. If you do, you're like a person who spends time arguing about the existence of the sun. Every human being knows there is a Creator. Some—those the Bible calls "fools"—deny that inner knowledge:

> The fool has said in his heart, "There is no God." (Psalm 14:1)

> For since the creation of the world His invisible attributes are clearly seen, being understood by the things that are made, even His

eternal power and Godhead, so that they are without excuse, because, although they knew God, they did not glorify Him as God, nor were thankful, but became futile in their thoughts, and their foolish hearts were darkened. Professing to be wise, they became fools. (Romans 1:20–22)

Don't Ignore the Will to Live

If you have a car, no doubt you have an owner's manual for it. If you're anything like me, you don't bother reading the owner's manual until something goes wrong. A red light appears on your dash, and the manual shows you how to fix it. Every human being should see a red light indicating something is seriously wrong with this world. We're all going to die. The Bible, God's owner's manual, tells us that the reason we will die is because we have sinned against God but that this can be fixed by trusting in the Savior.

When I ask questions such as, "Do you think there's an afterlife?" "Do you think about your death?" and "Are you afraid to die?" I'm drawing their attention to the red light. I tell sinners they have a serious problem: they are going to die and should be doing everything they can to find an answer to death. They should be searching the Scriptures, earnestly praying, and asking questions. I want them to be alarmed, and I want their will to live (their fear of death) to cause them to open their hearts to the gospel.

Don't Stay with the Carnal Mind

Romans 8:7 shows us an uphill path that is full of thorns: "The carnal mind is enmity against God; for it is not subject to the law of God, nor indeed can be." The "carnal mind" is a reference to the sinful mind of the unregenerate. Their thoughts are against God. They are enemies of God in their minds: "And you…were alienated and enemies in your mind by wicked works" (Colossians 1:21).

When we stay in the realm of apologetics, arguing about the existence of God, the validity of the Bible, the theory of evolution, and so on, we are staying in that area of hostility. Notice that Scripture tells us exactly where that hostility is directed: "The carnal mind is enmity against God." Sinners are offended by God's moral government. They don't want God telling them what to do. The Scriptures call sinners "the children of disobedience" (Colossians 3:6, KJV). They love sin, and the Ten Commandments are a threat to their darling pleasures.

To effectively reach the lost with the gospel, we must move away from that carnal, rebellious mind, and the way to do that is to do what Jesus did. He directed the conversation to the work of the Law (see Mark 10:17–19), which is already written in the heart. He addressed the conscience—rather than the intellect—using the moral Law. Every human being intuitively knows that the Ten Commandments are true and right, even the obscure one about keeping the Sabbath holy. We know this because the Jews have the physical Law written in stone, and the Gentiles have the same Law written in their hearts, their conscience bearing witness (see Romans 2:15). In other words, the conscience affirms the truth of each of the commandments. Therefore, do what Jesus did—take aim at the conscience. Stir it up to do its God-given duty.

Don't Be Afraid to Produce Fear

When Jesus was on the cross, those who have no fear of God often point to His supposed public admission that He was a fraud:

> Now from the sixth hour until the ninth hour there was darkness over all the land. And about the ninth hour Jesus cried out with a loud voice, saying, "Eli, Eli, lama sabachthani?" that is, "My God, My God, why have You forsaken Me?" (Matthew 27:45,46)

There you have it. The wicked claim that a confused and disappointed Jesus suddenly realized that God wasn't with Him. Darkness had covered the land for three hours, and now the lights had been turned back on, making it clear that He was an imposter. What's more, this sad admission wasn't even whispered. Jesus said it in a loud voice.

It's understandable that those who hate God latch on to this saying and come to their erroneous conclusion. But the Scriptures give us light on what took place. The Bible says that God is holy and cannot look upon evil:

"My God, My God, why have You forsaken Me?" (Matthew 27:45,46)

You are of purer eyes than to behold evil,
And cannot look on wickedness. (Habakkuk
1:13)

We are also told that sin causes a separation between sinners and God:

Behold, the LORD's hand is not shortened,
That it cannot save;
Nor His ear heavy,
That it cannot hear.
But your iniquities have separated you from
    your God;
And your sins have hidden His face from you,
So that He will not hear. (Isaiah 59:1,2)

When the Lamb of God was on the cross, this wasn't just a substitutionary sacrifice. He wasn't only stepping into our place. He actually *became* sin for us. Think of the nature of sin—of murder, rebellion, adultery, anger, greed, rape, jealousy, hatred, lust, theft, and so on—as one mass of seething and dark evil. Jesus became *that* for us: "For He made Him who knew no sin *to be sin for us*, that we might become the righteousness of God in Him" (2 Corinthians 5:21).

The psalmist had prophesied that the Messiah would cry out these very words, and that He would do so because God is holy and couldn't look upon such evil. God separated Himself from the suffering Savior: "My God, My God, why have You forsaken Me?...*But You are holy*" (Psalm 22:1,3).

By attempting to accuse the Savior of sin, skeptics stand on their own oxygen hose. They have to face Him on Judgment Day, and on that Day there will be deadly silence (see Matthew 22:12); they will have no justification for their sin. What a fearful thing!

There are certain fears for which we should be thankful. We should be fearful of fire, fearful of vicious dogs, and so on. In these cases, fear is our friend, not our enemy. And the fear of the Lord, according to the Scriptures, is the beginning of wisdom (see Psalm 111:10). Those who don't fear God haven't begun to be wise. Our aim should be to set sinners on the path of wisdom. We should put the fear of God in them, and the way to do that is to open up the Ten Commandments as Jesus did and combine that with future punishment:

> Truly, these times of ignorance God overlooked, but now commands all men everywhere to repent, *because* He has appointed a day on which He will judge the world in righteousness. (Acts 17:30,31)

> Now as he [Paul] reasoned about righteousness, self-control, *and the judgment to come*, Felix was afraid. (Acts 24:25)

> "And do not fear those who kill the body but cannot kill the soul. But rather fear Him who is able to destroy both soul and body in hell." (Matthew 10:28)

Never talk about the reality of Hell before you open up the Law. Hell makes no sense unless sin is understood to be exceedingly sinful. That's the function of the Law:

> What shall we say then? Is the law sin? Certainly not! On the contrary, I would not have known sin except through the law. For I would not have known covetousness unless the law had said, "You shall not covet."… Therefore the law is holy, and the commandment holy and just and good…Has then what is good become death to me? Certainly not! But sin, that it might appear sin, was producing death in me through what is good, so that sin through the commandment might become exceedingly sinful. (Romans 7:7,12,13)

Don't Forget the Cross

It sounds a little crazy to say not to forget to preach the cross, but it's very common for it to be overlooked. Again, the Scriptures say that the gospel is the power of God to salvation (see Romans 1:16), and the very heart of the gospel is Christ on the cross. If we leave that out of our message, we give sinners a placebo. It will be of no benefit to them because they will hear a message that does not show them the righteousness of God or the mercy of God in Christ.

Don't Resort to the Sinner's Prayer

When I was a new Christian (nearly fifty years ago), I did great damage to the cause of the kingdom by leading prospective converts in the unbiblical "sinner's prayer." This modern method is perhaps the number one reason the contemporary church is filled with false converts (tares among the wheat and goats among the sheep) and why 80–90 percent of those who come through this method fall away from the faith. We mock the Pharisees for their unbiblical traditions yet cling dearly to this unbiblical tradition.

Do you remember how the Pharisees were offended when their tradition was challenged? Are you? Perhaps you're thinking, *But what about all those who were genuinely saved who prayed the sinner's prayer?* I address that issue in a book called *God Has a Wonderful Plan for Your Life: The Myth of the Modern Message*. The cover picture is of Stephen being stoned to death. Evangelist Bill Fay, author of *Share Jesus Without Fear*, said this of my book: "While reading this book my heart went into atrial fibrillation; it's *that* good! After I finished it, I couldn't sleep. There's nothing like it. It is truly from God. I gave it to my researcher. After reading it, he was so excited he was ready to get on a plane, take it to pastors and make them read it while he sat there."[6]

Todd Friel, host of Wretched TV and Wretched Radio, said after reading it: "This book is explosive.

Eye opening. Jaw dropping. Staggeringly helpful. In other words, this book is classic Ray Comfort. If you grieve over the statistical fact there are more rotten fish than good fish in the Evangelical Church, this book will forever change the way you present the gospel."[7]

You can read for free the short book *God Has a Wonderful Plan for Your Life* at FreeWonderfulBook. com.

Also, take a moment to watch this very short clip: tinyurl.com/az7cev28.

Then please listen to "Hell's Best Kept Secret" at the bottom of the homepage at LivingWaters.com.

These resources will challenge almost everything you believe about how to reach the lost. I say these things not to offend you but in the hope that a very strayed church will return to the way Jesus reached the lost.

In the next chapter, we will look at how you can potentially reach millions with the gospel.

CHAPTER 6

HOW TO START YOUR OWN YOUTUBE CHANNEL

The Scriptures tell us that when Jesus spoke of His thirst during the crucifixion, He was fulfilling Messianic prophecy:

> After this, Jesus, knowing that all things were now accomplished, that the Scripture might be fulfilled, said, "I thirst!" (John 19:28)

Eight hundred years earlier, David looked to this moment when he penned these words about the Messiah:

> My strength is dried up like a potsherd,
> And My tongue clings to My jaws;
> You have brought Me to the dust of death.
> (Psalm 22:15)

When Jesus, who is often referred to as "the son of David," cried out in thirst on the cross, we are reminded that David too once cried out in thirst:

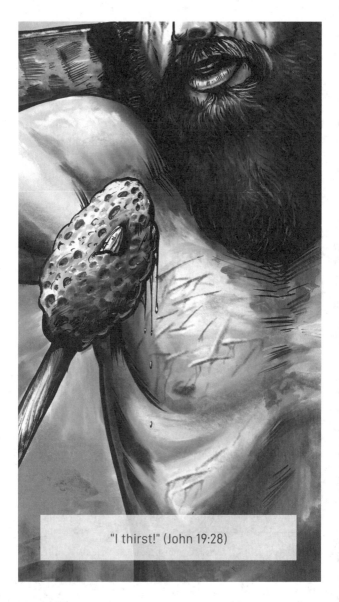

"I thirst!" (John 19:28)

And David said with longing, "Oh, that someone would give me a drink of the water from the well of Bethlehem, which is by the gate!" (2 Samuel 23:15)

This dying world thirsts for the water from the well of Bethlehem. Only Jesus can give them living water (see John 7:38). That's what we bring them in the gospel.

One of the most effective ways to reach the world with the gospel is through YouTube. Our Living Waters YouTube channel is at present approaching two hundred million views. We are forever thankful to God for opening this door into the hearts of millions. But we're not special. Never let small beginnings discourage you; every tree started with a tiny seed. Our channel started small. I held up a camera with one hand, a microphone with the other, and shared the gospel. In a matter of ten years, we passed over one hundred million views. Imagine if I had said that I was a nobody who couldn't do this and that no one would be interested. The way to achieve nothing is to do nothing.

Imagine filming beautiful sunrises, or all the different trees, dogs, or birds in the world, or you cooking your favorite recipes. Then bounce from those topics to a Bible verse, or talk about the One who creates birds, dogs, and trees and makes the sun rise. Pray that God gives you wisdom and creativity.

Or you can simply do what I do—interview people about what they think happens after death. I film with an iPhone which has a plug-in black Sennheiser Handmic Digital Dynamic Handheld Microphone.

California law says that a person should be eighteen or older or have parental permission to be on camera. Following is my typical approach:

RAY: Excuse me. Would you like to be on YouTube? I ask people if they think there's an afterlife. What do you think?

STRANGER: I don't know.

RAY: Do you think about it much?

STRANGER: I do actually. Maybe we come back as something else. I don't know.

RAY: What's your name?

STRANGER: Cathy.

RAY: Cathy, if you will let me interview you for five or ten minutes, I'll give you a five-dollar gift card as a thank you. Okay?

CATHY: Okay.

RAY: Thanks for being a good sport. What do you do for a job?

CATHY: I'm an editor.

RAY: Do you like your job?

CATHY: Yes, it's great, and I get to meet really nice people.

RAY: I'll need to ask your permission to do this.

The small talk about her job is to give me time to turn the camera on and plug in the microphone. It also helps her to feel more relaxed. I frame her on my phone, making sure I have a pleasant background with no bright lights behind her and that I'm in a low-noise area if possible. I then double-check that the camera is on and the microphone is firmly plugged in.

RAY: Cathy, can I have permission to film you for YouTube and for all media purposes?

CATHY: Sure.

RAY: Cathy, do you think there's an afterlife?

It's not easy to get people to come on camera. Some days I am turned down by twenty to thirty people in a row. But I don't give up. I keep asking until I get one.

Let me share something that's a little personal. As I ask people to come on camera, I hand them a card with a picture of Sam on the bike (available at LivingWaters.com). If they turn me down, I say, "If you will give me a five-minute interview on what you think about the afterlife, I'll give you a five-dollar gift card to In-N-Out" (everyone in California knows about their wildly popular hamburgers). If they say, "No, thank you," I give them the gift card anyway. Without exception, people who were standoffish melt in a second. I don't mention the interview again because I don't want the gift to look like a bribe. I want them to know that I really care about them.

As I ride away, I imagine them later biting into a burger, thinking about this complete stranger who for no apparent reason gave them that gift. I know that if someone randomly did that for me, I would go to their YouTube channel and watch their videos. That person would already have credibility with me. That's why I really don't mind being turned down. It certainly is more blessed to give than to receive.

In the hope that I've sparked your interest in filming an interview, I am going to share some principles that will help you grow your channel.

Grabbing the Ears

On May 1, 2018, we posted an interesting video called *Dogs Can Talk—Full Christian Movie*. I was excited because it contained the gospel and videos of cute dogs doing cool things. But it took a long three years to get just one hundred thousand views. I expected it to get that many views in weeks. So I reedited it and we rereleased it on July 3, 2021, with the new title *If You're a Christian, This Is Why You Need a Dog*. It passed one hundred thousand views in just twelve days!

The difference was that I used FTTT—four principles that I have learned over the years.

1. Fluff. I edited out any fluff. I removed anything that didn't cut to the chase within the first ten seconds. This is because of what social media and modern living has done to us. Years ago, I would sit in front of an old movie and think nothing of a two-minute introduction. It would show the title. The actors. The type of film used. The type of color used for the film. Who scored the music. Who created the wardrobe. Who collaborated in writing the script. But nowadays I immediately get impatient because I have been programmed to get things quickly. If a video doesn't deliver something exciting within seconds, we click out and move on. So anything that slows that process has to be cut.

2. Teaser. Every successful TV program doesn't break for advertisements without some sort of teaser. They will say something to hook your interest in what's coming up after the break. If you are normal, your curiosity will be stirred enough to make you want to stay. For example, if you're watching a show about motorcycles, they may say something like, "Who invented the first motorcycle in 1885? Was it William Harley, Henry Ford, or Gottlieb Daimler?"

Do you know the answer? Find out in the next chapter. (Just kidding. I wouldn't do that to you. You can find out right now.) But it does show how powerful a good teaser can be to make us curious. (It was Daimler.)

Because of its ability to stir us, some sort of teaser should replace the fluff, along with "Coming up" written on the screen.

3. Title. A good title is absolutely essential. Consider the two I mentioned earlier: *Dogs Can Talk— Full Christian Movie* and *If You're a Christian, This Is Why You Need a Dog.* The old title simply makes a statement and is bland. The new one contains a challenge. It says that I'm not cutting the mustard. I'm falling short of what I should be as a Christian. *But why?* There's the curiosity stirrer—the hook. *Why* do I need a dog?

A good title should aim to contain controversy, conflict, or curiosity. Take, for example, one video clip we made that rocketed to millions of views very quickly. It was titled *He Didn't Care about God…but Was in Tears after Hearing This*. Hearing *what*? He didn't care, but then he did. Why? *I have to find out!* Another provocative and, therefore, successful title we used was *She Laughs at First…Then the Preacher Says This*. Why did she laugh? What was it that the preacher said?

Can you see the conflict, the controversy, and the curiosity in these titles? They grab us by the ears.

4. Thumbnail. The picture that accompanies the upcoming video is like a movie poster. It should be an eye-candy teaser and depict a strange expression, a cute dog, an unusual or colorful hairstyle—anything that will provoke a second look.

Ready to Preach the Gospel

If you want to use a camera to interview people but you still feel nervous or inadequate, I'm going to share something that you won't want to miss because it will certainly be helpful.

A person who thinks honey will be found in a wasp nest is either ignorant or a fool. Mess with a nest and the odds are that wasps will chase you and possibly sting you to death. When a well-known man of God is publicly found to be engaged in sexual sin, media wasps will chase him into his home, into his ministry, and then sting and stun his faithful followers. So many leaders have fallen away from the faith in modern Christianity that we have almost become accustomed to it. Almost.

Early in 2021, a brilliant and popular apologist was found to have lived a secret life of sexual sin, and his fall carried a particularly painful sting because his name was synonymous with integrity. He was the gentleman's gentleman, the proud mountain of intellectualism to which we pointed as evidence that Christianity wasn't just for the fool on a hill.

Yet at the same time, his amazing eloquence had always concerned me. We had him speak at one of our conferences years ago, and I was very impressed with his fluency. But at the same time, I had a private concern. I often expressed that disquiet in a self-deprecating way by saying that I listened to him in awe but came away not having a clue what he had just said. I even addressed my concern (in fear and trembling) in one of my books. I say "fear and trembling" because I didn't want to come across as judgmental or as harboring some sort of secret jealousy because of his popularity.

The big lesson we should all take from this is to listen to our eloquent apologists and ask ourselves, Are they preaching about sin, righteousness, and judgment? Are their secular hearers being impressed with grandiloquence (I used that word to impress you), or are they being awakened to their terrible danger? Do they tremble as did Felix after hearing Paul preach (see Acts 24:25)?

Intellectual preaching often produces intellectual converts who name the name of Christ but don't depart from iniquity; they are strangers to the new birth. Each of us should ask ourselves whether we had been talked into our faith or had encountered the living God. If we came through the door of argument, then all it will take is a better argument to cause us to leave by another door. Take to heart Paul's warning about such so-called conversions:

> And I, brethren, when I came to you, did not come with excellence of speech or of wisdom declaring to you the testimony of God. For I determined not to know anything among you except Jesus Christ and Him crucified. I was with you in weakness, in fear, and in much trembling. And my speech and my preaching were not with persuasive words of human wisdom, but in demonstration of the Spirit and of power, that your faith should not be in the wisdom of men but in the power of God. (1 Corinthians 2:1–5)

We are called to be witnesses of Christ. Judges aren't concerned about the eloquence of a witness. They just want to hear the simple truth, the whole truth, and nothing but the truth. And the truth is in Jesus. It is in Christ crucified for the sin of the world. Fail to preach that ultimate truth, and we are not true and faithful witnesses. We will end up with a hung jury.

Let's talk about the subject of apologetics and our inadequacy in this context. We should use apologetics as is commanded in 1 Peter 3:15: "But in your hearts honor Christ the Lord as holy, always being prepared to make a defense [Greek *apologia:* a formal written defense of one's opinions or conduct] to anyone who asks you for a reason for the hope that is in you; yet do it with gentleness and respect" (ESV).

But notice what it was that Paul was ready to defend: "Knowing that I am appointed for *the defense of the gospel*" (Philippians 1:17).

We aren't particularly to defend God's existence, the inspiration of the Bible, or the church. We are to defend the gospel. In Romans 1, Paul makes his agenda clear: "For God is my witness, whom I serve with my spirit in the gospel of His Son.... I am ready to preach the gospel.... For I am not ashamed of the gospel of Christ" (Romans 1:9,15,16).

We should be ready to defend the gospel. Again, apologetics have their place, but we have a problem when we elevate them above the gospel and never preach the actual good news of salvation. And here is my point: all this is good news for those of us who lack eloquence. We don't need it. We are ready to go right now.

In the next chapter, we will look at a difficult question skeptics may ask and how to respond to them.

CHAPTER 7

DIFFICULT QUESTIONS AND THOSE WHO ASK THEM

You may not realize it, but you *are* gifted. You have been gifted with everlasting life (see Romans 6:23), so share that gift with others. Pass it along. And don't forget your "bait." If you don't have a dog to warm hearts, use your smile. A warm smile coupled with a "Good morning!" can attract the attention of a stranger.

Practice how you greet a stranger. There's a greeting that sounds like you've been forced to say it, and then there's a "Good morning!" given in a tone that says you really do care about the person. It carries warmth. Strive for that greeting. Have a gospel tract ready and say, "Did you get one of these?" Don't identify what it is as you reach out your hand to give it to them. You want to use curiosity to get them to take it. It's okay to use this method because Jesus used it with the woman at the well. He said to her, "If you knew the gift of God, and who it is who says to you, 'Give Me a drink,' you would have asked Him, and He would have given you living water" (John 4:10).

Jesus' words provoked her interest (see v. 15). It stirred her curiosity about this living water, and your "Did you get one of these?" will do the same thing.

Rarely will you be asked difficult questions in person. But with the advent of the Internet, sinners can access lists of "gotcha" questions for Christians. These are questions that they believe cannot be answered. Here's one I was asked online: Why is picking up sticks on the wrong day serious to God but offering your daughters to a mob to be gang-raped isn't?

The first part of the question is a reference to a terrifying incident in Scripture:

> Now while the children of Israel were in the wilderness, they found a man gathering sticks on the Sabbath day. And those who found him gathering sticks brought him to Moses and Aaron, and to all the congregation. They put him under guard, because it had not been explained what should be done to him.
>
> Then the LORD said to Moses, "The man must surely be put to death; all the congregation shall stone him with stones outside the camp." So, as the LORD commanded Moses, all the congregation brought him outside the

camp and stoned him with stones, and he died. (Numbers 15:32–36)

What follows was my response.

Great question. Violation of God's Law always brings capital punishment. "The soul who sins shall die" (Ezekiel 18:20). "The wages of sin is death" (Romans 6:23). Like this man, you too will die because you have violated God's Law—with your lust, blasphemy, lying, theft, greed, and so on. That man was stoned because he was rebellious, and you will find that the same thing will happen to you if you continue to rebel against God: "And whoever falls on this stone will be broken; but on whomever it falls, it will grind him to powder" (Matthew 21:44).

The "stone" spoken of in this verse is Jesus Christ. If you refuse to fall on that stone (to trust Him), it will fall on you and grind you to powder. When something is ground to powder, a thorough job is done. Nothing is left. God's judgment will be so thorough on Judgment Day that nothing will be left unpunished. Every lustful thought, every deed done in darkness, every idle word spoken will be exposed and brought to justice. Here's a glimpse of that fearful day "when the Lord Jesus is revealed from heaven with His mighty angels, in flaming fire taking vengeance on those who do not know God, and on those who do not obey the gospel of our Lord Jesus Christ. These shall be punished with everlasting destruction from the presence of the Lord and from the glory of His power" (2 Thessalonians 1:7–9).

Why was that man punished immediately, and you are not? The Scriptures tell us the answer. God is patiently waiting, "not willing that any should perish but that all should come to repentance" (2 Peter 3:9). But don't mistake His patience for complacency, approval, or divine ignorance. Every time you sin, you are storing up more of His wrath:

> Do you despise the riches of His goodness, forbearance, and longsuffering, not knowing that the goodness of God leads you to repentance? But in accordance with your hardness and your impenitent heart you are treasuring up for yourself wrath in the day of wrath and revelation of the righteous judgment of God, who "will render to each one according to his deeds": eternal life to those who by patient continuance in doing good seek for glory, honor, and immortality; but to those who are self-seeking and do not obey the truth, but obey unrighteousness—indignation and wrath, tribulation and anguish, on every soul of man who does evil, of the Jew first and also of the Greek; but glory, honor, and peace to everyone who works what is good, to the Jew first and also to the Greek. For there is no partiality with God. (Romans 2:4–11)

It will do you no good to be concerned about that man in the Old Testament. Instead, have concern about your own precious life—your salvation—because you are also in terrible danger.

The second part of your question is in reference to Lot (see Genesis 19:4–8). Lot was a thoughtless man who offered his daughters to a group of angry homosexuals. His absurd suggestion never came to pass—mainly because homosexuals aren't interested in raping women. But what he did was not as dumb as what you are trying to do. God is offering you everlasting life, and you are trying to justify your porn addiction by pointing out obscure incidents in Scripture that happened thousands of years ago.

(Im)moral Relativists

There is nothing new under the sun. Scripture tells us that Adam tried to justify himself by blaming God for his transgression. He said that the woman God gave to him was to blame (see Genesis 3:12). Modern-day Adams will do the same thing. So don't talk to them when they're hiding behind a bush. Use the stick of God's Law to flush them out into the open. Speak directly to their sinful heart and show them the danger they're in. Let them know they cannot hide from God and that God "will bring every work into judgment, including every secret thing, whether good or evil" (Ecclesiastes 12:14).

One common way contemporary Adams do battle is to use a weapon called "relativism." According to *Encyclopedia Britannica*, relativism is "the doctrine that there are no absolute truths in ethics and that what is morally right or wrong varies from person to person or from society to society."[8]

The Bible gives a clearer definition:

Every way of a man is right in his own eyes,
But the LORD weighs the hearts. (Proverbs 21:2)

There is a similar well-known and much-quoted verse in Judges 17:6. But verse 5 gives us a better perspective. Here it is in full: "The man Micah had a shrine, and made an ephod and household idols; and he consecrated one of his sons, who became his priest. In those days there was no king in Israel; everyone did what was right in his own eyes."

Micah had his own handmade gods. The Bible calls these "dumb" idols (see 1 Corinthians 12:2) because they don't speak. And it's very convenient that these gods are silent about sin. Idolatry means you can determine what's morally right in your own eyes. It allows you to pray to your god and at the same time kill a child in the womb. It means you can snuggle up to your sweet little god and at the same time snuggle up to an attractive individual and commit adultery. Idolatry accommodates sin.

And there sit moral relativists. They have their own concept of what God is like. Maybe they think He doesn't exist. Perhaps their god is unknowable or happy about sin or ignorant or unjust. Or their god might be just plain immoral and have a small crowd of virgins waiting for vicious male killers:

In August, 2001, the American television channel CBS aired an interview with a Hamas activist Muhammad Abu Wardeh, who recruited terrorists for suicide bombings in Israel. Abu Wardeh was quoted as saying: "I described to him how God would compensate the martyr for sacrificing his life for his land. If you become a martyr, God will give you 70 virgins, 70 wives and everlasting happiness." Wardeh was in fact shortchanging his recruits since the rewards in Paradise for martyrs was 72 virgins.[9]

Whatever the case, the sinner's imagination opens the doorway to moral relativism. And arguing with relativists is like trying to swim against a riptide. Nothing they say is defined, and if you let them, they will sink you in an ocean of insincere rhetoric and subtle semantics.

Pilate's question, "What is truth?" was probably rhetorical (see John 18:38). Had he addressed the question to Jesus in earnest, he may have gotten an answer. Those who resort to relativism don't want an answer. They want to hide from God so they can indulge in their darling sins. They suppose that it provides a hiding place for them. To reach them with the gospel, you have to lift them up onto the solid rock of the moral Law. That's the only absolute that matters. Again, you must move away from the carnal mind—the mind that is in a state of enmity against God (see Romans 8:7).

This isn't a game. It's a life and death issue—theirs. Because the *lost* aren't earnest about their salvation, *you* must be. They are sinking into death, and if they won't reach up their hand to yours, you must reach yours down to theirs (see Jude 23). And that process begins with your earnest words.

Perhaps the greatest errors the unsaved make when it comes to God are their beliefs that (1) God is good, (2) they are good, and (3) their good will outweigh their bad if there's a Judgment Day.

God certainly is good. This seems to be the error of the rich young ruler (see Mark 10:17). He tossed around the word "good" like a frisbee at a church picnic, not knowing that it is a pin-pulled hand grenade. How do we define good? Is a man good because he's never raped a woman? Some might say that he is. But is he good if he *desired* to rape a woman but didn't because he was afraid of getting caught? Are individuals good because they're pacifists and would never go to war? Or are they good because they go to war to defend their beloved country?

It comes back to the definition of "good." Sinners usually agree that God is good, and they assume that because He is good He will overlook their sins. But the thing they are hoping will save them on Judgment Day is the very thing that will condemn them. If God is good, He must punish all evil.

God's demands leave no room for relativism. "Be perfect" is the requirement of the Law (see Matthew 5:48). That means absolute moral perfection in thought, word, and deed. The Law is violated by desire. It counts hatred as murder and lust as adultery (see 1 John 3:15; Matthew 5:28). Every time we sin, we store up its outrage.

To reach lost sinners you must put them in the dock, standing before the Judge of the universe and His perfect Law (see Psalm 19:7). You must give them a little taste of Judgment Day—and pray that it leaves the bitter taste of death in their mouth. That's what Jesus did with the rich young ruler, and it sent him away sorrowful (see Mark 10:17–22).

In the next chapter, we will look at something amazing that God has placed in you that will remain dormant until needed.

CHAPTER 8

YOU CAN LIFT THE CAR

If you've ever seen a commercial for United Airlines, you are almost certain to be familiar with George Gershwin's composition *Rhapsody in Blue*. I was once watching a pianist play the nine-minute composition when I noticed something that put me in awe. He was playing it by memory. *Rhapsody in Blue* is incredibly complex, yet this pianist had his eyes closed most of the time. That is, for nine minutes his fingers hit multiple keys at the precise second and the correct thrust perhaps ten thousand times.

In an article titled "Science Says Piano Players' Brains Are Very Different from Everybody Else's," the author says:

> Pianists are born (like all of us) with one side of the brain being favored more than the other. This is not unusual; everyone has a natural preference for which hand we prefer holding our pen in or eating our cereal with (from

a young age). The difference here is that pianists begin practicing using both parts of the brain when mastering the use of each hand whilst playing.

If one hand were to be weaker than the other, playing the piano would not work. Without skill in both it can end up sounding clunky and unbalanced, at best. This necessity to practice and to master both hands means that the brain effectively evens itself out. With practice, despite each player having a naturally stronger hand when they begin, by the time they have become an expert, the weaker hand is strengthened to the same degree as the stronger one.[10]

The pianist's mind had to not only retain every note but also recall them and perfectly imitate them on the keys, never hitting a wrong note. I was thrown into wonder, not at the pianist's ability to play so skillfully, but at the power of God to create him with that ability. How could He fashion around eighty-six billion neurons with each neuron communicating with many others to form circuits and share information? It hurts my brain to think such thoughts. Medical researcher Floyd E. Bloom stated:

As we begin the 21st century, the Hubble space telescope is providing us with information about as yet uncharted regions of the universe and the promise that we may learn something about the origin of the cosmos. This same spirit of adventure is also being directed to the most complex structure that exists in the universe—the human brain.[11]

To paraphrase "How Great Thou Art," oh Lord, my God, when I in awesome wonder consider all the brains Thy hands have made... God didn't just make and assemble eighty-six billion living neurons when He created pianists' brains. He did the same thing with *your* brain, the brains of billions of people, and the distinctly different brains of bees, cats, horses, dogs, fish, birds, giraffes, fleas, elephants, and a million and one other living creatures. Add to that the fact that you and I as human beings have the unique ability to consider all the brains His hands have made. It seems that none of the animal kingdom are able to think about the amazing works of God and be left in awesome wonder.

The ability to consider God's wonders is the doorway to worship, a window into the fear of God, and the impetus for genuine humility—because it puts God in His rightful place and us in ours. Seeing Him in His greatness rids us of the sin of pride. It changes everything. Brilliant piano players, gorgeous flowers, amazing birds, the magnificent sun, and the vast blue sky will never look the same when the Maker is painted into the picture. Doing so will turn mountainous problems into molehills because it explodes our faith in God.

With these lofty thoughts tucked safely into the brain, look at these wonderfully wise words penned by Solomon in his wisdom:

> My son, if you receive my words,
> And treasure my commands within you,
> So that you incline your ear to wisdom,
> And apply your heart to understanding;
> Yes, if you cry out for discernment,
> And lift up your voice for understanding,
> If you seek her as silver,
> And search for her as for hidden treasures;
> Then you will understand the fear of the
>   LORD,
> And find the knowledge of God. (Proverbs
>   2:1–5)

While the world seeks riches and power, we seek what God esteems. We set our heart to gain wisdom, understanding, and discernment. Incline your ear, apply your heart, cry out, and lift up your voice and you will then understand the fear of the Lord and find the knowledge of God. That's the treasure we seek because it brings us to the right knowledge of what God is like.

When Job was experiencing terrible suffering and deep depression, he said some things that missed the mark. When God spoke to him, He said:

> "Who is this who darkens counsel
> By words without knowledge?" (Job 38:2)

Those words perfectly sum up the erroneous philosophy of this world. Scripture paints it as being deceitful: "Beware lest anyone cheat you through philosophy and empty deceit, according to the tradition of men, according to the basic principles of the world, and not according to Christ" (Colossians 2:8).

And that empty deceit comes because of words that are without knowledge. This evil world is a field of blood where the dead bury the dead. It can add nothing to us when it comes to the knowledge of God. As Scripture says, "Blessed is the man who walks *not* in the counsel of the ungodly" (Psalm 1:1).

Oh, how precious it is to have the Word of God as a lamp to our feet and a light to our path. His Word is truth and something on which we can hang our hat. It gives us a right understanding of our Creator. Read with confidence the psalmist's inspired and inspirational revelation:

> O LORD, You have searched me and known
>   me.
> You know my sitting down and my rising up;
> You understand my thought afar off.
> You comprehend my path and my lying down,
> And are acquainted with all my ways.
> For there is not a word on my tongue,
> But behold, O LORD, You know it altogether.
> You have hedged me behind and before,
> And laid Your hand upon me.
> Such knowledge is too wonderful for me;
> It is high, I cannot attain it. (Psalm 139:1–6)

Great Exploits

Here now is my belabored point. A right understanding of the power of God is both mind-blowing
and at the same time consoling. The Creator has
given us precious promises so that we can achieve
great things for His glory: "Those who do wickedly
against the covenant he shall corrupt with flattery;
but the people who know their God shall be strong,
and carry out great exploits" (Daniel 11:32).

It doesn't matter that we can't sing or dance or
play the piano. He isn't impressed with the most
gifted of human beings. Why should He be when He
is the One who gifted them? But He *is* impressed
with faith. It pleases Him (see Hebrews 11:6). Jesus
marveled when a Roman centurion exercised faith in
Him: "When Jesus heard it, He marveled, and said to
those who followed, 'Assuredly, I say to you, I have
not found such great faith, not even in Israel!'"
(Matthew 8:10).

A friend once asked my opinion about the
meaning of Ephesians 4:11: "And He Himself gave
some to be apostles, some prophets, some evange-
lists, and some pastors and teachers." My friend said:

> I'm studying this passage for a sermon. I rec-
> ognize that we are all called to share the gospel
> and I agree with your analogy of "having the
> gift of feeding starving children." However, the
> verse says that Jesus gifts the Church. Would
> you agree that some people are particularly

gifted with an extra dose of compassion, ability to share the gospel, burden for the lost, easiness to "evangelize," etc., just as some are particularly gifted as teachers?

It is true that there are some who are more eloquent than others. They are confident and never get tongue-tied. They are comfortable speaking to strangers. They have a God-given ability to retain knowledge, and so on. They are naturally gifted and therefore find evangelism easier than someone who doesn't have those gifts. However, God tells us to ask for what we need: "If you then, being evil, know how to give good gifts to your children, how much more will your Father who is in heaven give good things to those who ask Him!" (Matthew 7:11). When we ask God for a gift that we may do His will (seeking the wisdom and knowledge He esteems), we are exercising faith, and that pleases Him. We are asking because we fear Him and want to do His will:

> He does not delight in the strength of the
> horse;
> He takes no pleasure in the legs of a man.
> The LORD takes pleasure in those who fear
> Him,
> In those who hope in His mercy. (Psalm
> 147:10,11)

Immediately after Jesus spoke about asking God for gifts in Matthew 7, He used the word *therefore* to link with a profound truth: "Therefore, whatever you want men to do to you, do also to them, for this is the Law and the Prophets" (v. 12).

When we ask God to help us to reach the lost, we are putting the Golden Rule into practice. We are loving our neighbors as ourselves. We are empathizing with their fearful future if they die in their sins. If I was blinded by sin and heading for Hell, I would want to be warned. Whatever you want others to do for you, do also for them. So don't be discouraged by your seeming inability. Let your lack be the impetus to plead with God for His help. I plead daily with the Lord to make me wise, particularly to reach the lost. In fact, I go for broke. This is the essence of what I pray almost every day:

> Father, please give me wisdom. Make me the wisest man on earth when it comes to reaching the lost. Teach me how to reach them, what to say, and how to say it. I don't want wisdom to be rich or famous or for power or for the praise of men. I am simply horrified that anyone would be damned in Hell. So please give me wisdom on how to reach them. In Jesus' name I pray.

Pray something like that with importunity and before you know it, you will be doing things you thought you never would.

In May 2021, a lone police officer in Virginia was hailed as a hero after body-cam footage was shared of him single-handedly lifting an overturned car off a woman as her child screamed for help:

> "The driver was laying underneath the vehicle with her head pinned by the sunroof....Seeing the trauma her child was witnessing, Deputy J. Holt went into overdrive. Through sheer will and determination... [he] was able to physically lift the vehicle up enough for the driver to maneuver her head out to safety."
>
> In the video, Holt...can be heard straining vigorously.[12]

What is so moving about the footage is that the officer can be heard yelling with pain—like a weight lifter who is lifting a weight that is way too heavy for him. *But he does it!* He couldn't let that woman die! If compassion gave that officer the ability to lift that vehicle off a dying woman, God's love can help us with the weight of reaching this dying world. It can help us do something we would normally be incapable of doing.

The following email came to our ministry:

> My wife was at the eye doctor while I stayed in the car reading *How to Win Souls and Influence People* [available at LivingWaters.com] again. I was on the topic of fear when the receptionist came outside and stood in front of my car. I could sense [God] urging me to do more than continue reading. As I continued reading, she walked into the parking lot (to my relief) but

then returned and lit up a cigarette. I stepped out in faith with the Curved Illusion tract[13] and asked her if it was break time. I showed her the illusion. She said the blue one is bigger. "And now?" I asked. Her mouth dropped open and I handed it to her, telling her there's a gospel message on the back. She gave a heartfelt thank you, finished her cigarette, and went back inside.

A few moments later my wife returned, revealing what happened when the receptionist went back inside. She enthusiastically told all of her associates, "Hey, look what this dude just gave me!" She then showed each of the employees and told them there was Scripture on the back. One of them was a young college student who refused to believe they were the same size, and took pictures of the tract with his phone. Needless to say, I gave my wife more illusions to give to each employee and she took a Big Money tract for the receptionist's child. I was so encouraged. Thank you, Living Waters, for this ministry, and whatever you do, don't leave home without your tracts! You just never know. —Kurt P.

The Cry of Eternity

The Scriptures exhort us to "serve the LORD with gladness" (Psalm 100:2). In my youth, I wasn't outwardly evil, but in my heart I loved that which God says is evil. When I reached my early twenties, I was enjoying life. But at the same time, I was quietly in despair, realizing how futile this life is with death waiting for each of us. As I read through the Sermon on the Mount, I suddenly understood that I had broken the Commandments, and saw my desperate need of God's mercy. The moment I put my trust in Jesus, I was saved from death's grip—giving me a reason to live. I had something I could pour my heart and soul into that was meaningful. To say that I serve the Lord with gladness is a gross understatement. I am forever humbled, unspeakably joyous, explosively thankful, and utterly grateful that God allows me to serve Him.

My wife and I have a small greenhouse made of heavy clear plastic in which we often place and hatch Monarch butterfly cocoons. One day I saw a Monarch in a corner, flapping its wings in an obvious panic. It instinctively knew to fly toward the light but was hindered from doing so by the plastic. So I took the butterfly gently in my hand, went outside, and let it fly into the heavens.

And so it is with you and me. We intuitively know that this world is not our home. It's full of evil, and it has unending pain and suffering. We groan within ourselves, waiting for the redemption of our bodies. We don't have a death wish; rather, it's a life wish—a longing for what we were created for. It's the cry of eternity in our hearts, put there by God. We know the day will come when the hand of God will either take us through the veil of death or come in power to take us home. There we will find a new heaven and a new earth where righteousness dwells and where we will have pleasure forevermore. We have God's promise on that—and there's nothing surer than God's Word.

Meanwhile, we continue to groan. Sometimes this longing comes on us like a cloud of depression. Our soul is cast down to the point that we despair of life. This is the precious well from which we draw empathy as we pray for the lost.

In the final chapter, we will look at the final words of some famous people and glean that which will help us to reach the lost.

CHAPTER 9

LAST WORDS OF FAMOUS PEOPLE

Just before Jesus dismissed His spirit, He said, "It is finished!" (John 19:30). It is only three words, yet they are the most profound words ever uttered by a human voice. Look at their Greek meaning:

> Of the last sayings of Christ on the cross, none is more important or more poignant than, "It is finished." Found only in the Gospel of John, the Greek word translated "it is finished" is *tetelestai*, an accounting term that means "paid in full." When Jesus uttered those words, He was declaring the debt owed to His Father was wiped away completely and forever. Not that Jesus wiped away any debt that *He* owed to the Father; rather, Jesus eliminated the debt owed by mankind—the debt of sin.[14]

I am forever in awe of Spurgeon's sanctified eloquence. Look at how he makes alive that dying moment on the cross:

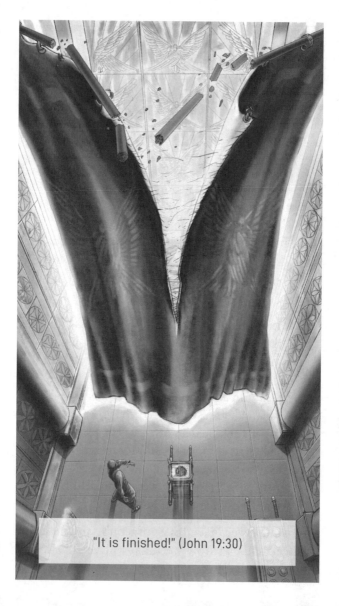

"It is finished!" (John 19:30)

The Son of God has been made man. He has lived a life of perfect virtue and of total self-denial. He has been all that life long despised and rejected of men, a man of sorrows and acquainted with grief. His enemies have been legion; his friends have been few, and those few faithless. He is at last delivered over into the hands of them that hate him. He is arrested while in the act of prayer; he is arraigned before both the spiritual and temporal courts. He is robed in mockery, and then unrobed in shame. He is set upon his throne in scorn, and then tied to the pillar in cruelty. He is declared innocent, and yet he is delivered up by the judge who ought to have preserved him from his persecutors. He is dragged through the streets of that Jerusalem which had killed the prophets, and would now crimson itself with the blood of the prophets' Master.

He is brought to the cross; he is nailed fast to the cruel wood. The sun burns him. His cruel wounds increase the fever. God forsakes him. "My God, my God, why hast thou forsaken me?" contains the concentrated anguish of the world. While he hangs there in mortal conflict with sin and Satan, his heart is broken, his limbs are dislocated. Heaven fails him, for the sun is veiled in darkness. Earth forsakes him, for "his disciples forsook him and fled." He looks everywhere, and there is none to help; he casts his eye around, and there is no man that can share his toil. He treads the winepress alone; and of the people there is none with him. On, on, he goes, steadily determined to drink the last dreg of that cup which must not pass from him if his Father's will be done. At last he cries—"It is finished," and he gives up the ghost. Hear it, Christians, hear this shout of triumph as it rings to-day with all the freshness and force which it had eighteen hundred years ago! Hear it from the Sacred Word, and from the Saviour's lips, and may the Spirit of God open your ears that you may hear as the learned, and understand what you hear![15]

After Jesus had drunk the last drop of the cup of suffering, He died. This was the climax of the final act in this horrific drama, just before the curtain was drawn. The face of God had turned toward Him, and His ear was open to Jesus' final prayer just before He breathed His last: "Father, 'into Your hands I commit My spirit'" (Luke 23:46).

There are no words to express the dismay we feel at the suffering we've just witnessed. But how we thank God for the unspeakable gift to come because of it! Death has forever lost its sting.

For years I have collected the last words of some famous people, hoping to someday write a book on the subject. I've decided instead to put them into the last chapter of this book because they are so applicable. Forget that these individuals were once famous. My hope is that the rawness of their words will speak to you as much as they have to me. I have called them "raw" because these are the naked final words of common human beings who have died. The thin façade of fame was dropped at the moment these precious mortals passed from this life. Such thoughts bring me to tears. They remind me that fame and fortune don't insulate any of us from this appointment with death.

My hope is that you don't gloss over these words, that you don't read them with the superficial morbid fascination with which we might glance at a tabloid headline. Take the time to think about the fate of each person who died in their sins. Read each one with the same sobriety you would have walking through a Holocaust museum. Stop for a moment and consider why he or she would say such things. Imagine the look in their eyes, hear the tone of their voice, and think what awaited them as they passed through the veil. Then let your thoughts foster a deep compassion for those who are still alive.

Let's begin with something wonderfully positive:

"See in what peace a Christian can die."

—Joseph Addison, writer, d. June 17, 1719

"Nothing, but death." (when asked by her sister, Cassandra, if there was anything she wanted)

—Jane Austen, writer, d. July 18, 1817

"I am not the least afraid to die."

—Charles Darwin, d. April 19, 1882

"How were the receipts today at Madison Square Garden?"

—P. T. Barnum, entrepreneur,
d. April 7, 1891

"Is everybody happy? I want everybody to be happy. I know I'm happy."

—Ethel Barrymore, actress,
d. June 18, 1959

"Die? I should say not, dear fellow. No Barrymore would allow such a conventional thing to happen to him."

—John Barrymore, actor, d. May 29, 1942

"Friends applaud, the comedy is finished."

—Ludwig van Beethoven, composer,
d. March 26, 1827

"Josephine."

—Napoleon Bonaparte, French emperor,
d. May 5, 1821

"Ah, that tastes nice. Thank you."

—Johannes Brahms, composer,
d. April 3, 1897

"Oh, I am not going to die, am I? He will not separate us, we have been so happy." (spoken to her husband of nine months, Rev. Arthur Nicholls)

> —Charlotte Bronte, writer,
> d. March 31, 1855

"Beautiful." (in reply to her husband who had asked how she felt)

> —Elizabeth Barrett Browning, writer,
> d. June 28, 1861

"Now I shall go to sleep. Goodnight."

> —Lord George Byron, writer,
> d. April 19, 1824

"I am still alive!" (stabbed to death by his own guards, as reported by Roman historian Tacitus)

> —Gaius Caligula, Roman emperor,
> d. January 24, AD 41

"Ay Jesus."

> —Charles V, king of France,
> d. September 16, 1380

"I'm bored with it all." (before slipping into a coma; he died nine days later)

> —Winston Churchill, statesman,
> d. January 24, 1965

"I have tried so hard to do the right."

> —Grover Cleveland, US president,
> d. June 24, 1908

"Goodnight my darlings, I'll see you tomorrow."
—Noël Coward, writer, d. March 26, 1973

"Don't you dare ask God to help me." (to her housekeeper, who had begun to pray aloud)
—Joan Crawford, actress, d. May 10, 1977

"What's happened?"
—Diana (Spencer), princess of Wales,
d. August 31, 1997

"It is very beautiful over there."
—Thomas Alva Edison, inventor,
d. October 18, 1931

"No, I shall not give in. I shall go on. I shall work to the end."
—Edward VII, king of Britain,
d. May 6, 1910

"Come my little one, and give me your hand." (spoken to his daughter, Ottilie)
—Johann Wolfgang von Goethe, writer,
d. March 22, 1832

"All my possessions for a moment of time."
—Elizabeth I, queen of England,
d. March 24, 1603

"I've never felt better."
—Douglas Fairbanks Sr., actor,
d. December 12, 1939

"I'd hate to die twice. It's so boring."

> —Richard Feynman, physicist,
> d. February 15, 1988

"A dying man can do nothing easy."

> —Benjamin Franklin, statesman,
> d. April 17, 1790

"Turn up the lights, I don't want to go home in the dark."

> —O. Henry (William Sidney Porter), writer,
> d. June 4, 1910

"All is lost. Monks, monks, monks!"

> —Henry VIII, king of England,
> d. January 28, 1547

"I am about to take my last voyage, a great leap in the dark."

> —Thomas Hobbes, writer,
> d. December 4, 1679

"Oh, do not cry—be good children and we will all meet in heaven."

> —Andrew Jackson, US president,
> d. June 8, 1845

"I see black light."

> —Victor Hugo, writer, d. May 22, 1885

"Why do you weep? Did you think I was immortal?"

> —Louis XIV, king of France,
> d. September 1, 1715

"I am a Queen, but I have not the power to move my arms."

> —Louise, queen of Prussia,
> d. July 19, 1810

"Let's cool it, brothers." (spoken to his assassins, three men who shot him sixteen times)

> —Malcolm X, Black leader,
> d. February 21, 1965

"Go on, get out—last words are for fools who haven't said enough." (to his housekeeper, who urged him to tell her his last words so she could write them down for posterity)

> —Karl Marx, revolutionary,
> d. March 14, 1883

"Nothing matters. Nothing matters."

> —Louis B. Mayer, film producer,
> d. October 29, 1957

"I love you, Sarah. For all eternity, I love you." (spoken to his wife)

> —James K. Polk, US president,
> d. June 15, 1849

"I am curious to see what happens in the next world to one who dies unshriven." (giving his reasons for refusing to see a priest as he lay dying)

—Pietro Perugino, Italian painter, d. 1523

"Lord, help my poor soul."

—Edgar Allan Poe, writer, d. October 7, 1849

"Sister, you're trying to keep me alive as an old curiosity, but I'm done, I'm finished, I'm going to die." (spoken to his nurse)

—George Bernard Shaw, playwright, d. November 2, 1950

"I have offended God and mankind because my work did not reach the quality it should have."

—Leonardo da Vinci, artist, d. May 2, 1519

"I die hard but am not afraid to go."

—George Washington, US president, d. December 14, 1799

"Go away. I'm all right."

—H. G. Wells, novelist, d. August 13, 1946

"I am ready."

—Woodrow Wilson, US president, d. February 3, 1924

"Father, 'into Your hands I commit My spirit'" (Luke 23:46)

And finally (as we saw earlier), the greatest of the last words ever spoken: "And when Jesus had cried out with a loud voice, He said, 'Father, "into Your hands I commit My spirit."'" Having said this, He breathed His last" (Luke 23:46). Once again, Jesus was fulfilling Scripture. In Psalm 31 we read, "Into Your hand I commit my spirit; You have redeemed me, O LORD God of truth" (v. 5).

May we be ever mindful of the seven last sayings of Jesus. If we allow them to, they can help spur us on in our endeavor to reach the lost. They remind us of His love and mercy toward the unsaved and of the assurance He gives us of our own salvation. They cause us to remember to honor our parents, to keep our faith in God despite our feelings in the midst of trials. We must never forget that He suffered thirst so that we could drink of the waters of life, that He finished the work so that we could rest from our labors. And of course, we remember how even death itself bowed the knee to Jesus of Nazareth. He was in total control then, and He is in total control now.

In conclusion, consider this incident that took place in June 2020:

> A blind woman who was banned from a Rhode Island park after sharing her Christian faith with others will be able to return to the park, following litigation. Last year, Gail Blair was barred from entering Westerly Library and Wilcox Park by the Rhode Island Memorial

and Library Association, which controls the public property.[16]

Fortunately, attorneys from First Liberty Institute stood up to this association, and she is once again allowed to talk about her faith at the park.

Gail Blair is blind, and yet she clearly sees the lost. She longs for them to see Him who is invisible. One would think that her condition would excuse her from the difficult task of evangelism. But it doesn't. What is *our* excuse today for not doing the same? Are we too shy? Too busy? Too fearful? Too lazy? Are we going through serious trials? Are we nailed to a cross?

It is my hope and prayer that something I've said in this little book has been helpful to you in your Christian walk and that you too will go ahead and use what you have to reach the lost.

God bless you.

Ray Comfort

NOTES

1. Karen B. London, "Dogs in Advertising," The Bark, March 2015, thebark.com/content/dogs-advertising.

2. "Spurgeon's Verse Expositions of the Bible: Luke 23," StudyLight.org, studylight.org/commentaries/eng/spe/luke-23.html.

3. Dick Harfield, "Is There Any Evidence That Jesus Sinned?," Quora, quora.com/Is-there-any-evidence-that-Jesus-sinned.

4. "Thieves, the Two on the Cross," McClintock and Strong Biblical Cyclopedia, biblicalcyclopedia.com/T/thieves-the-two-on-the-cross.html.

5. If you don't know what tracts to choose, you may like our Starter Kit. It contains fifty aluminum coins with the Ten Commandments on one side and the gospel on the other, one hundred "Are You a Good Person" comic tracts, one hundred copies of "101 of the World's Best One Liners," and one hundred "Million Dollar Bill" tracts.

6. Ray Comfort, *God Has a Wonderful Plan for Your Life* (Bellfower, CA: Living Waters Publications, 2010), available at LivingWaters.com.

7. Ibid.

8. James Rachels, "Ethical relativism," *Encyclopedia Britannica*, britannica.com/topic/ethical-relativism.

9. Ibn Warriq, "Virgins? What Virgins?," *Guardian*, January 11, 2002, theguardian.com/books/2002/jan/12/books.guardianreview5.

10. Daniel Owen van Dommelen, "Science Says Piano Players' Brains Are Very Different from Everybody Else's," Lifehack, lifehack.org/517069/science-says-piano-players-brains-are-very-different-from-everybody-elses.

11. "Floyd E. Bloom Quotes," AZ Quotes, azquotes.com/quote/579978.

12. Tim Fitzsimons, "Video Shows Virginia Deputy Lifting Car to Save Trapped Woman," *NBC News*, May 20, 2021, nbcnews.com/news/us-news/video-shows-virginia-deputy-lifting-car-save-trapped-woman-n1268038.

13. You can see the amazing Curved Illusion tract at our website, Living Waters.com.

14. "What Did Jesus Mean when He said, 'It Is Finished'?," Got Questions, gotquestions.org/it-is-finished.html.

15. "It Is Finished!," Spurgeon Center, spurgeon.org/resource-library/sermons/it-is-finished.

16. Michael Gryboski, "Blind Woman Banned from Rhode Island Park Over Sharing Christian Faith Can Return," *Christian Post*, October 30, 2020, christianpost.com/news/woman-banned-from-rhode-island-park-over-sharing-faith-returns.html.

RESOURCES

Please visit our website where you can sign up for our free weekly e-newsletter. To learn how to share your faith the way Jesus did, don't miss these helpful resources:

- *God Has a Wonderful Plan for Your Life: The Myth of the Modern Message* (our most important book)

- *Hell's Best Kept Secret* and *True & False Conversion* (you can listen to these vital messages free at LivingWaters.com)

- *Basic Training Course* (evangelism DVD study)

- *Tough Questions* (apologetics DVD study)

- *Anyone But Me*

- *What* Did *Jesus Do?*

- *How to Bring Your Children to Christ… & Keep Them There*

- *The Way of the Master for Kids*

- *Out of the Comfort Zone*

- *World Religions in a Nutshell*

You can also gain further insights by watching the *Way of the Master* television program (WayoftheMaster.com).

For Non-Christians

If you have not yet placed your trust in Jesus Christ and would like additional information, please check out the following helpful resources:

How to Know God Exists. Clear evidences for His existence will convince you that belief in God is reasonable and rational—a matter of fact and not faith.

Made In Heaven. Discover how the most innovative ideas of modern human ingenuity are actually features borrowed from the amazing work of God in creation.

Why Christianity? (DVD). If you have ever asked what happens after we die, if there is a Heaven, or how good we have to be to go there, this DVD will help you.

See our YouTube channel (youtube.com/livingwaters) to watch free movies such as "The Atheist Delusion," "Evolution vs. God," "Crazy Bible," as well as thousands of other fascinating videos.

If you are a new believer, please read "Save Yourself Some Pain," written just for you (available free online at LivingWaters.com, or as a booklet).

For more resources, visit LivingWaters.com, call 800-437-1893, or write to: Living Waters Publications, P.O. Box 1172, Bellflower, CA 90707.

THE EVIDENCE STUDY BIBLE

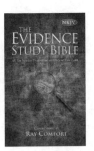

"An invaluable tool for becoming a more effective witness."
—FRANKLIN GRAHAM

The Evidence Study Bible arms you not just with apologetic information to refute the arguments of skeptics, but with practical evangelism training on how to lead them to Christ.

- Discover answers to over 200 questions such as: Why is there suffering? Where did Cain get his wife? How could a loving God send people to hell? What about those who never hear of Jesus?

- In addition to thousands of verse-related comments, over 130 informative articles will help you better comprehend and communicate the Christian faith.

- Over two dozen articles on evolution will thoroughly prepare you to refute the theory.

- Dozens of articles on other religions will help you understand and address the beliefs of Mormons, Hindus, Muslims, Jehovah's Witnesses, cults, etc.

- Hundreds of inspiring quotes from renowned Christian leaders and practical tips on defending your faith will greatly encourage and equip you.

The Evidence Study Bible provides powerful and compelling evidence that will enrich your trust in God and His Word, deepen your love for the truth, and enable you to reach those you care about with the message of eternal life.